Narrow Seas, Small Navies,
and
Fat Merchantmen

Narrow Seas, Small Navies, and Fat Merchantmen

Naval Strategies for the 1990s

Charles W. Koburger, Jr.

PRAEGER

New York
Westport, Connecticut
London

V
163
K64
1990

Library of Congress Cataloging-in-Publication Data

Koburger, Charles W.
    Narrow seas, small Navies, and fat merchantmen: naval
strategies for the 1990s / Charles W. Koburger, Jr.
        p.   cm.
    Includes bibliographical references.
    ISBN 0-275-93557-4 (alk. paper)
    1. Naval strategy.   2. Sea control.   3. Coast defenses.
    4. States, Small.   5. Sea-power—United States.   6. United States.
    Navy.   I. Title.
    V163.K64 1990
    359'.03—dc20   90-31579

British Library Cataloguing-in-Publication Data is available.

Library of Congress Catalog Card Number: 90-31579
ISBN: 0-275-93557-4

First Published in 1990

Praeger Publishers, One Madison Avenue, New York, NY 10010
An imprint of Greenwood Publishing Group, Inc.

Printed in the United States of America

The paper used in this book complies with the
Permanent Paper Standard issued by the National
Information Standards Organization (Z39.48-1984).

10 9 8 7 6 5 4 3 2 1

*To the U.S. Coast Guard—the lifesavers and the law
on the sea, now celebrating 200 years of service.*

*The conclusions and opinions contained herein are
those of the author alone, and do not necessarily
reflect those of anyone else in the whole world.*

Contents

Photographs follow page 83.

Naval Abbreviations and Acronyms

AA	Anti-aircraft (and missile)
ACV	Air-cushion vehicle
AEW	Airborne early warning
ARAPAHO	Containerized kit for conversion of container ships and tankers into V/STOL carriers
AS-12	French light air-to-surface missile
ASW	Anti-submarine warfare
AWACS	Airborne warning and control system
Blue water	High seas, open ocean
Brown water	River and estuarine
CAP	Combat air patrol, the defensive air umbrella
CIWS	Close in weapons systems
COOP	Craft (fishing boats, tugs, offshore oil service boats) of opportunity taken up for minesweeping duty
COTP	Captain of the Port
DD	Destroyer
ECM	Electronic countermeasures (jammers and decoys)
EEZ	Exclusive economic zone

EW	Electronic warfare
EXOCET	French guided missile with air-to-surface, surface-to-surface, and coast defense variants
FAC	Fast attack craft
FF	Frigate
GABRIEL	Israel anti-ship missile, surface-to-surface
HARPOON	U.S. surface-to-surface missile
HARRIER	British V/STOL fighter-bomber
HAWKEYE	U.S. naval AWACS (E-2C)
Helo	Helicopter
IFF	Identification, friend or foe
IMO	International Maritime Organization
INMARSAT	International Maritime Satellite
IR	Infra-red
KOMAR	Soviet FAC, carrying two STYX
LAMPS	U.S. ASW Helo
LCM	Landing craft, medium
LCU	Landing craft, utility
LPG	Liquid petroleum gas
LST	Landing ship, tank
MO8	WWI Anglo-Russian moored mine
MDZ	Maritime defense zone
MARISAT	*See* INMARSAT
MAVERICK	U.S. air-to-surface missile
MSO	Marine safety officer
NATO	North Atlantic Treaty Organization
NCS	Naval control of shipping
OCMI	Officer-in-charge, marine inspection
OSA	Soviet FAC, carrying four STYX
PHALANX	U.S. CIWS
RAF	Royal Air Force
RN	Royal Navy
S-boat	German FAC

SEA KILLER	Italian surface-to-surface missile
SEA KING	British ASW helicopter
SEA STAL-LION	U.S. helicopter
SILKWORM	Chinese version of STYX missile
Skunk	Surface contact, unknown
SLOC	Sea line of communication
STO/VL	Short take-off, vertical landing
STYX	Soviet anti-ship missile, surface-to-surface
SUPER-ETEN-DARD	French carrier fighter-bomber
TOMAHAWK	U.S. cruise missile
TRACKER	U.S. carrier fixed-wing AWCS plane (S-2F)
U-boat	Submarine (German)
USCG	U.S. Coast Guard
VHF-FM	Short-range (horizon) voice radio
V/STOL	Vertical/short takeoff and landing
VTS	Vessel traffic system
White Water	Inshore
WWI	First World War
WWII	Second World War

Introduction

TAKING DEPARTURE

This book focuses on the smaller navies and on their threat to superpowers. Ignorance of and disinterest on the part of U.S. naval authorities in violence in the narrow seas is—with several striking exceptions—proverbial. Our continued unpreparedness for such war-fighting results, each time such emergencies arise, in long delays before we are able to react effectively, and most recently in a somewhat embarrassing call for help to reluctant allies. This will no longer do.

As one element of the great pulsing stream of world political affairs, two old but previously separate threads in naval strategy and tactics seem to be coming forcefully together today. The result has been a revolution in naval affairs, and a major shifting in the balance of seapower.

The first of these threads is the role of the narrow seas in maritime strategy, the second, that of the world's lesser navies in these waters.

Navies today tend to divide themselves into three groups: super-navies (the United States and the Soviet Union); medium navies, if we have to separate them; and the lesser others. The super-navies have world-class status. The medium navies are those smaller navies of strong regional value. The others are primarily of local worth. It is primarily these last which we are looking at here.

Most naval thought is Mahanian, or post-Mahan.[1] It is written for large "blue water" big ship, big gun, high seas navies vying for command of the sea during the first half of the twentieth century. The decisive battle, total blockade, the fleet in being, convoy, all these concepts are familiar to us. Fought in relative isolation on the open sea, what was described was *naval* war.[2]

War in the narrow seas is not fought in isolation, but, rather, close to land, where everything and everybody is likely to be involved all the time. All waters are inshore waters, from one shore all the way across to the other. For our merchantmen as well as naval vessels, what is the actual *maritime* threat?[3] How can we best handle it?

SEAPOWER TODAY

Seapower is defined as the military ability to influence events at sea, and from the sea. Seapower has an infinite number of gradations, running from that exercised by the smallest far-off military-maritime coast guard to that of a super-navy. Enough of those kinds of power most suited to the problem at hand leads to command of the sea. The concept is best known as Mahan's, of course.

Ultimately, it is the surface of the sea that is the great prize. We may fight under the sea and over it (as well as on it) in war. We trade on it, we fly over it, we fish it, we get oil and gas from it, and we mine it, in peace. But all of these activities depend in the end on at least a minimum of surface control in war—enough for coastal defense, minelaying and sweeping, and coastal convoys—and on freedom of the seas, in peace. These last "lawful occasions" are what seapower really aims to defend.

In the most general terms, the instruments of maritime power are time, space, and resources. In the narrow seas, times are compressed and distances are short. A twenty-minute run from base to target is common. Even for a small navy, resources involve numbers multiplied by skill.

In a short war, these assets tend to be a given. They are at least initially what they are. A longer war gives opportunity to change them, or some of them, at any rate. In the end, what you have is the original fleet plus new building and purchases, less losses, all modified by fresh recruitment, training, and leadership, and the development of bases.

It is only in the twentieth century that seapower has really been satisfactorily defined, and its corollaries worked to their logical conclusion. That having been done, the ground began to erode right from under Mahan's tidy big navy, big ship, big gun, blue water ideas. Nonetheless, as late as 1940 conventional naval thought was dominated by his governing hypotheses. Navies in those days were rated automatically by the number of their battleships. For those that had big navies, these were heady (and endlessly comforting) ideas. How they have had to be modified—and why—we shall now see.

In the narrow seas, modern technology—especially that concerning V/STOL and shore-based air power, fast attack craft, submarines, missiles, and mines—can achieve sea denial without requiring superior surface naval forces. This has tended to deprive traditional seapower of its ability to command narrow seas adjacent to enemy-held lands. To do so requires of it the expenditure of quite inordinate assets, for questionable gain.

Dramatic improvements in the range, accuracy, and destructive power of relatively light, compact, cheap precision-guided munitions make it possible today for even the smallest navies to contest effectively anyone's unwelcome presence off its coast.

In these waters, a lesser navy's nuisance value or damage quotient against even the most powerful can be large enough to raise materially the threshold of war.

Unless it enjoys overwhelming command of the sea, big ship traditional seapower can for any significant period of time dominate only those waters distant from enemy naval and air bases. The accelerating effect of technology has taken away its ability to impose a blockade or any other continuous exercise of power, close in.

Mahan emphasized the importance of the narrow seas, and of their control. He also emphasized the necessity thereto of potential for close and continuous blockade. For seapower, this poses a serious dilemma. The naval world has been turned upside down.

THE NEW ERA

In the narrow seas, more often than not, it is the bordering small navies which now call the tune to which the super-navies dance. It is they who determine who shall pass and the price he shall pay. This book examines at length the impact of these small navies on the ships, planes, and tactics of those big navies.

All of this was foreshadowed a century ago with the development of the torpedo and its platforms—the torpedo boat, the submarine, and the airplane. Then came the mine and the missile. As exploited, all of these developments materially lessen the freedom of the Great Powers to sail the narrow seas, and correspondingly increase the ability of even the smallest littoral states to control what takes place in their contiguous waters.

These navies become critical players on the world stage in three fundamentally different kinds of situations:

1. Lesser states warring against neighbors: Israel fought both Syria and Egypt at once (1973), Turkey occupied Turkish (northern) Cyprus (1974), Iraq invaded Iran (1980);

2. Lesser states acting against extra-regional powers: Israel moved against the United States' *Liberty* (1967), North Korea seized the United States' *Pueblo* (1968), Libya attacked units of the Sixth Fleet (repeatedly, during the 1980s);

3. Outsiders acting against lesser states: the United States in the Eastern Mediterranean (in various contexts, since 1947), the United States in North Korea (1950–53), the United States in Vietnam (1965–73).

In the last two cases, the United States is the major player. We were, however, definitely not alone. Britain and France, for instance, also had roles, and not just with the joint Anglo-French attempt to re-seize the Suez Canal (1956). Britain faced Iraq in Kuwait (1961), Indonesia in Northern Borneo (1962–66), and Argentina in the Falklands (1982). France seized Haiphong (1946) and supported its Indochinese war for ten years (1945–54), and patrolled off Algeria (1954–62).

Events in the Persian Gulf (1980–88) only validate everything that has been written about the narrow seas, and bring it all up to date. During the course of this century's two world wars, nowhere in the Baltic did the sea escape the influence of the land, nor did the land that of the sea. Although gulf operations took place half a century later, and even though gulf operations incorporated the most recent weaponry (including missiles), the same truth held.

The ability and readiness of lesser states, particularly those along the narrow seas, to challenge larger powers has been strengthened by a host of recent developments: the current emphasis on the sovereignty and rights over the duties of states; the use of "self-defense" as a cover for the most flagrant violations of customary international law; the control of the United Nations' General Assembly by the lesser states; the speed and comprehensiveness of modern media. It is a long list, and the trend is probably irreversible.

So, with the Balkanization of the world and the proliferation of arms and armies throughout the world, a large number (40) of small but significant national naval forces has grown. An even larger group (100) could be at least intermittently dangerous—if they were enemies.

In these small navies, there are few conventional flat-deck aircraft carriers or nuclear-powered submarines. Ship types tend to be down-sized, across the board. If they do have a carrier, it will be a V/STOL one. They replace destroyers with fast attack craft. They pay for this in comparative radius of action and in sea-keeping ability—neither of great interest in most narrow seas, it should be noted.

Small navies can now use their new maritime power to disrupt important patterns of international trade. Used against the Great Powers as they pass, these small navies can have an impact far out of proportion to their size. Roles are being redefined. Strategies are being revised to reflect this.

Second, quasi-navies (coast guards) are appearing in many areas. There may in fact be more of them than there are real fighting navies. How so? Until the middle of this century, control of coastal waters in peacetime by military-maritime forces large or small consisted mainly of policing fishing, whaling, and sealing in a few sensitive areas; of preventing smuggling and illegal immigration; and of standby search and rescue. The task was doable, part-time, by traditional navies per se, without interfering unduly with their other tasks. In most cases, they were left with it.

Today that mission is a full-time job. The new nation-states have extended their control over huge areas of their frontier seas called exclusive economic zones (EEZs), as have the older states. There has been an explosive growth of large tanker traffic. Air and sea rescue take up ever more time. Smuggling, illegal immigration, terrorism, and unwanted intelligence-gathering activities all add to the problem. Coastal waters have become dangerous, and they require policing by experts. More and more, this task has been turned over to specialized coast guards, either alongside or in place of navies. These maritime police must be viewed as an integral part of the overall naval scene.

NECESSARY PAPERWORK

As the world becomes increasingly Balkanized, it keeps threatening to become unglued. The lesser navies are therefore of greater interest than ever before. It seems they appear on the front pages of everyone's newspaper, if you notice, every day, but present no clear image. Such an image can be drawn. We do it here.

There is much evidence of what is going on today in the naval world but one searches in vain for some genuine key to what it all means. This we attempt to give.

This book provides definitions of the common naval concepts—sea control, sea denial, for instance—that one often meets. Those concepts are presented in nontechnical terms, for the general reader.

Lesser navies are thus here defined as those other than the

two super ones. All of them are of at least some local maritime utility. A few possess regional stature. A few are of alliance value, and may be tailored particularly to their alliance role. All possess trouble-making potential far beyond that indicated by their size.

Most of these small navies operate in one of the narrow seas. Past failures in these waters should make a study like this of continuing politico-military value.

This book is divided into three main parts. The first part, Chapters 1 and 2, looks at those navies which rim the globe's narrow seas. The second part, Chapters 3–5, describes operations characteristic of those same small navies. The last part, Chapters 6 and 7, puts the first two together, and ends by outlining some of the implications of this modern naval revolution for superpower (U.S.) maritime strategy.

For us Americans, the prime user of strategic, technical, and tactical information is of course our navy. It follows that, insofar as possible, we should use its conceptual frame of reference. The wider reading public will have no trouble with such an approach, in any case. There is, of course, a difference on the order of many magnitudes in the size and mission of our navy as compared with those with which we shall deal here, but it is the underlying concepts that concern us most. These we can borrow and apply, properly modified, as long as we remember that purposes can sometimes be quite different from ours.

No attempt has been made here to catalogue every small example of the employment of lesser navies in our time. There are just too many examples—an average of probably one a year since 1936. Just listing all of them would make a book in itself.

The examples that were chosen are considered to demonstrate well a particular point. Several keep appearing because they have special relevance to recent U.S. experience. Others simply emphasize the point being made. Many were left out, nonetheless, to avoid swamping the reader with data. It is, after all, ideas that we are looking for.

This book is not a substitute for a true operational manual. Rather, it informs on the subject; it alerts; it challenges, it suggests. Otherwise it is of necessity incomplete, duplicating some elements of a manual, yes, but leaving others out and including some things not usually found in such a work. I trust that an adequate manual does somewhere exist. I have not seen it.

The Public Affairs Offices in Coast Guard Headquarters (Washington) and the Seventh Coast Guard District Office (Miami) repeatedly provided information, photographs, and other assistance, even while in the midst of crises of their own. Thanks.

Buried in this book are parts of my paper, "Swords and Surfboats," given at a maritime law enforcement seminar held in London in 1983. This seminar was organized jointly by the British Nautical Institute and *Navy International*, an independent journal of seapower. Thanks.

Scattered throughout this book is a good bit of other writing which first appeared at one time or another in *Navy International*. For the encouragement that journal has given me over the years, more thanks.

Captain Albert A. Schaufelberger USN (ret.) and Lieutenant Commander Glenn L. Simpson USNR (ret.) kindly agreed to read the manuscript in an earlier form. They made a number of constructive suggestions. Thanks.

If in this book I am able to see far, it is again because I stand on the shoulders of many tall men. The best of the authors on whom I drew are listed in the bibliography that appears at the end of the book. Thanks to them all, too. The mistakes are of course all mine.

The overwhelming U.S. power so characteristic of the post–World War II era is now considerably reduced. We Americans need to play smart as well as heavy. To continue to be ignorant of the narrow seas and careless of the way we sail them will be a costly error. We *can* play smarter.

NOTES

1. Mahanian: following and in accordance with the writings of Captain (later Rear Admiral) Alfred Thayer Mahan, USN. Mahan was the author of the seminal *The Influence of Seapower Upon History 1660–1783*, first published in 1890.

2. Naval war: war fought between opposing navies in relative isolation on the open sea, fleet against fleet.

3. Maritime war: war fought between opposing fleets, inshore, where everything and everybody is likely to be involved all the time.

Narrow Seas, Small Navies, and Fat Merchantmen

1

Navies

THE IDENTIFICATION PROBLEM

Although we do admittedly commence at a theoretical beginning, most of the navies belonging to states littoral to the narrow seas can best be described as lesser, even small. These are the "white water" (inshore) and their tiny cousins the "brown water" (river and estuarine) forces. These have until recently been little able to face large "blue water" (high seas) forces. In the narrow seas, this is no longer true. There the indigenous lesser navies are coming into their own. What do these lesser navies look like?

There are infinite gradations in military-maritime power. De facto, it starts with the least, the first harbor police unit, and proceeds through a marine constabulary or coast guard to a coastal patrol force, to a high seas navy. As such a force develops, it extends its reach and its ships grow in size, becoming more versatile, mirroring a parallel expansion of a state's interests. The conceptual progression is a natural one.

For this, however, names are seldom a totally useful guide. Police forces are quickly renamed navies, without any real change in function, simply for the prestige and perhaps future interest carried with it. Coast guards are sometimes civilian forces, not fighting units. Coast guards are called navies. Navies are called coast guards. Dealing with this problem requires examining the basic function of the force in question, never mind the name.

We shall deal here with the sea-based/sea-related naval warriors first, then with the others. This gives us a useful conceptual framework from which to categorize all these richly varied forces.

Otherwise, their real world function is seldom clear. What ought to be fundamental duties for the unit in question can in fact sometimes be ignored or bypassed, for a host of reasons locally considered adequate. Several incomplete military-maritime forces can overlay each the other, all of them too small and ill-trained to do their job. Efforts can be sporadic, intermittent, and, therefore, less than ineffective, only symbolic.

THE MIXED BAG

Small navies are a mixed bag. Over forty of these lesser dedicated war-fighting forces number small submarines in their armories, but they are always very few and the level of training may not be very high. Except for those of Britain and France, there are no nuclear submarines. Over fifty navies operate aircraft dedicated to or primarily for maritime roles, but in most cases these are shore-based. In-flight refueling is rare. With the exception of France's two, there are no major carriers. About sixty navies man vessels carrying surface-to-surface antiship missiles, typically short (horizon) range. Most of these are fast attack craft (FACs) the maximum action radius of which is not more than 200–300 miles from their bases. Over twenty units boast a formal mining capability, but almost anyone can lay them. Command, control, and communications are unlikely to be effective over more than the same distance from base.

Nonetheless, fully developed, all navies may be seen to have four generalized functions, which they carry out to a greater or lesser degree. These are:

1. maritime presence (coercive or supportive), indicating both interest and reach;

2. sea control/sea denial;

3. power (force) projection, to include landing troops, shore bombardment, and bombing; and

4. deterrence (tactical and strategic).

As they attempt to perform these four functions, the small navies divide themselves quite naturally into four fairly distinct classes:

1. the modern high-tech computerized, automated, fully mechanized native Western ones, like those of West Germany and Sweden;

2. the expensive Third World ones on which enough money has been lavished for them to have bought high-tech weaponry like that of Oman;

3. the relatively low-tech Third World ones that well reflect the indigenous societies from which they spring, like that of the Philippines; and

4. those which are not entirely one or the other, being very bad or very good, and which can always be an unpleasant surprise.

Today, the better small navies are reaching out. Once a 200 to 300–mile operating radius was the norm. Today it is 500 to 600 miles. Ship sizes are inching up. These navies train, too, long and hard. They are *led*.

ORGANIZATION

In principle, most small navies recognize two distinct organizational lines—an administrative one and an operational one. In the very smallest navies, these managerial lines may be one and the same, but normally they come together only at the top of the organizational pyramid.

Administratively, the chain of command formally begins at the chief executive. It runs from him through a cabinet-level officer—a secretary of defense or minister of the navy—to a chief of naval operations. He, in turn, has a staff of his own.

The executive staff will be made up of various directors: engineering, medicine, finance, the marine corps (if there is one).

Aircraft, if any, may come from an organic naval air arm. If not, they may only be under the navy's operational control, the planes coming from a separate unified air force.

Whatever the precise organization of these staffs, they are designed to perform the same basic duties. All exist to assist in formulating plans and in supervising execution of those plans. They establish doctrine, lay out unit organization and composition, ensure that the navy is ready to carry out its assigned tasks.

From the headquarters, the administrative chain extends to the shore element—much of which is run directly by the executive staff itself—and to the operating forces.

Operationally, the chain of command runs from a chief of naval operations to the shore element and to the operating forces: the fleet commander; base, air station, and area commanders; the commandant of the marine corps, and marine units.

From here, operational control tends to become tactical command. Out of the fleet's type squadrons (fast attack craft, escort, and mine; perhaps carrier, submarine, amphibious, and service) temporary task groups are formed to meet specific needs, tailored to fit the task at hand. Marines may be organized into units up to brigade in size, but ordinarily only a single company or a battalion will be amphibious-trained and complete with sea lift.

AIRCRAFT CARRIERS

Large modern navies are measured by the number of their conventional large-deck aircraft carriers. Carriers today, however, verge on being luxuries the smaller navies can no longer afford. Some are giving them up. Nonetheless, although relatively few can any longer boast a standard carrier of any size, if they are to fight wars of almost any kind—operations at almost any level—that is, of any kind beyond the support range of their shore-based dedicated air, this increasingly means they require "light" or "escort" V/STOL (vertical/short takeoff and landing) carriers. These they can afford.

In a high threat environment, if a continuous CAP (combat air patrol) over the fleet is not to be flown by its shore-based supporting air, the best that could be hoped for is that these fighters be on a strip alert.[1] Under these conditions, planes from an airfield 200 miles distant would take about twenty minutes from the call to arrive over the force. That seldom would be good enough to protect the force from serious losses. Under these conditions, a carrier must actually accompany the fleet.

Gaining in popularity are simple garage-type flat tops, single screw, displacing some 12,000 to 20,000 tons, with a maximum speed around twenty knots. They have no need for large angled decks, or steam catapults, or arresting gear. They are capable of operating a notional air group of some twenty planes, a mix of airborne early warning (AEW) (3) and ASW (9) helicopters and V/STOL fighter-bombers (8).

While V/STOL carriers are too small to handle standard high performance aircraft, they do not always operate in the V/STOL mode. As a matter of fact, V/STOL carriers usually operate in the STO/VL (short takeoff, vertical landing) mode. Vertical takeoff imposes severe penalties in terms of permissible takeoff weight on any plane. This translates into either limited range and short endurance, or restricted weaponry. Even a short roll (or required takeoff run) eases this quite a bit.

STO/VL operations are made even more effective by the use of the "ski-lift" ramp. With such a ramp, the takeoff roll of a fully loaded fighter-bomber is about half of what is demanded from a conventional deck. The planes can carry significantly more weight—ordnance or fuel—too.

Even smaller versions of these V/STOL carriers are now being built or are on the drawing boards, some less than half the average current size. These can carry some six fighter-bombers and perhaps four helos, but their small flight decks make steadily operating fixed and rotary-wing aircraft simultaneously much more of a chore. The planes' recovery and recycling area is just too small. These ships are necessarily shorter-legged, too.

There are still some conventional light carriers in service, however. Most were laid down in WWII for service in the U.S.

or Royal Navies, and later sold as surplus. Those that still have them are now faced with the fact that they are now old, needing expensive modernization or replacement. Some fleets are, therefore, opting out of carriers of any kind. Some few are continuing with this type, building new ones or refurbishing old ones.

France has two 30,000-ton conventional carriers, and is building two nuclear-powered 36,000-ton replacements.

The Argentines, however—with the Falklands war (1982) in mind—have just spent two years overhauling their former Colossus-class carrier *Veinticinco de Mayo*. At 16,000 tons, capable of 24 knots, she carries twelve Super-Etendard fighter-bombers, six Tracker ASW planes, and four Sea King helos.

Spain only recently built *Principe de Asturias*, a typical 16,000-ton V/STOL carrier, the first of perhaps two. Italy has built *Guiseppe Garibaldi*, a smaller (12,000-ton) version, also the first of perhaps two.

Whether it is light refurbished conventional or new V/STOL we are looking at, carriers are still not cheap. Possession of one or more is what marks a dominant regional power, more than anything else.

AIRCRAFT

Long usage has identified five functional roles for naval aircraft: as fighters, attack/strike planes, patrol planes, transports, and ASW planes. The development of the fighter-bomber tends to combine those two types. Similarly, some aircraft combine ASW and patrol functions. Maritime patrol planes and transports are similar, large-bodied and long-legged. Others overlap, too.

V/STOL carriers today carry fighter-bombers, AEW planes, ASW planes, fixed and rotary wing. There will be about twenty of them aboard a light carrier, in some combination, variable according to task.

These aircraft—land-based and/or carrier-borne—can project concentrated firepower directly into any sea or land area within range. Carrier-borne aircraft have operated successfully from shore bases. Except for V/STOL, the reverse is seldom—but not never—possible.

Underway at sea, every naval force employing organic aircraft will be covered by its own fighters. Strikes may be launched against a possible enemy. There will be an ASW screen, usually helos. There will be a reconnaissance element, perhaps land-based. The whole will be orchestrated by the force commander.

Airborne early warning (AEW) is a latecomer to V/STOL carriers. AEW planes do take up valuable space, displacing some of the ASW, or strike planes, or both. Even with just this rudimentary battle area management capability, however, embarked in whatever form, fighters can be twice or even three times as effective, and fewer fighters need to be taken on board.

For small navies, land-based airborne warning and control (AWACS) planes expand on this capability. So far without a V/STOL platform, the naval E-2C Hawkeye, for instance, can monitor a 238,000 square mile area. It can automatically track hundreds of targets against any background, land or sea. It can follow ships at sea down to patrol boat in size. It can locate and identify enemy radars to maximum line of sight range.

The E-2C's normal detection range of up to 250 miles, taking in everything from the surface up to 100,000 feet, extends air warning and reaction time to thirty minutes. This gives an AWACS controller time to alert and select the forces to counter any threat, to vector fighter and attack planes or ships to their most efficient intercept position. It gives the fleet a chance to upgrade its own area and point defense readiness to maximum (see Appendix C).

Integrating heavy, very long-range shore-based E-3A Sentry AWACS planes with the smaller E-2Cs, forming one master overall surveillance and control unit, can extend a naval force's horizon out to 600 miles.

As a rule, in these small navies, if there is a naval air arm at all, it will be land-based. This makes airborne in-flight refueling capabilities a serious, universal problem. Their absence is strongly felt.

Any investment in long-range maritime patrol planes should consider not only wartime reconnaissance and ASW but also peacetime EEZ surveillance and general police duties. But interservice rivalries, political expediency, and strategic myopia generally combine to kill such ideas. Both political and technical costs are always at stake.

Helicopters have proven the most useful of aircraft. They carry out short-range surveillance; close-in ASW; personnel transport ship-to-ship, between ship and shore, and shore-to-shore; vertical replenishment; search and rescue; medical evacuation. They are mean, agile gunships. They base interchangeably, at sea and ashore.

For the future, the Harrier V/STOL fighter—now subsonic—will become supersonic. AWACS will be fitted to the tilt-rotor V-22 Osprey, giving it V/STOL capability. AEW will accompany the fleet, enabling a force to take full advantage of the improved Harrier, facing land-based fighters on more like even terms. Versions of the V-22, all capable of taking off and rising like a helicopter, but flying straight and level twice as fast, twice as far, and then landing like a helo, requiring only half the maintenance, will replace helos in many operational roles.

GUIDED MISSILES

Guided missiles substitute for aircraft, rockets, bombs, and guns, strategically and tactically. It is the tactical use that interests us here. These tactical missiles can be classified as surface-to-surface, air-to-surface, air-to-air, or surface-to-air (AA). They are all subsonic, consisting of an airframe, motor, guidance, and warhead. Some are wire-guided, or beamriders. Others like the Styx, Gabriel, Harpoon, or Silkworm surface-to-surface missiles are "fire and forget," containing integral radar or infrared (heat-seeking) terminal homing.

In the Falklands (1982), while British vessels were certainly lost from bomb and rocket, it was the Argentine French-built Exocet that proved to be the most dangerous single weapon. The Exocet AM-39 is the air-to-surface version of this over-the-horizon sea-skimming cruise missile. It is a "fire and forget" 15.5-foot, 1440-pound missile, capable of being launched from a plane flying anywhere between 30,000 and 300 feet. It has a maximum range of 30 to 44 miles, depending on the altitude and speed of the launching platform.

To launch, the aircraft simply programs the Exocet with target range and bearing, obtained by popping up over the horizon for a quick look. The missile is then released, and the pilot heads back to base. The missile drops to five or six feet above the water, flying at just below the speed of sound (Mach 0.9). Eight miles from its target, the missile's own homing radar takes over. At roughly 12.5 miles a minute, Exocet is difficult to detect, worse to stop, the actual time of flight being measured only in seconds.

The Soviet-built Styx, the U.S. Harpoon, the Chinese Silkworm, and the Israeli Gabriel surface-to-surface missiles share the essential characteristics shown for Exocet. They fly at Mach 0.9. Styx and Harpoon are 15 feet long; the former has a 30-mile range, the latter a 60-mile one. Silkworm—developed from the Styx—has a 50-mile reach. The smaller Gabriel was originally limited to 12.5 miles, later lengthened to 22.

Larger conventionally armed sea-launched cruise missiles like Tomahawk (20 feet long, 3400 pounds, 350 miles at Mach 0.7) can be effective against not only shipping but also coastal targets like ports.

With all these missiles, when employed against over-the-horizon targets, it is usually necessary to use targeting systems external to the launching unit—helos, for example. Knocking them out blinds the missile.

FAST ATTACK CRAFT (FAC)

Lesser navies may not be rich enough to afford, or large enough to need aircraft carriers of any size. They may not possess submarines, or any of the other complicated high tech weaponry available on the market today. But one thing they will have will be fast attack craft (FACs). In some cases, FACs are all they have. FACs have become the backbone of most small navies.

FACs are relatively small, heavily armed craft, fast (40 knots or more) by any standards. They were developed in response to an obviously growing requirement for boats able to operate offensively in narrow, congested waters in the face of a heavy air threat, numerous coastal defenses, and 24-hour radar/ searchlight watch. Destroyer types had become too large for this kind of work.

These craft were first developed in mid-World War I, as 40- to 70-foot hydroplane-hulled coastal motor boats. They appeared concurrently in the British and Italian navies, both using them with great success, even against battleships in port.

Only the Germans, however, entered WWII with a coherent FAC doctrine and a practiced fleet of boats. They had used the interwar years to develop their *Schnellboote* (S-boats), big (114-foot) 100-ton, displacement-hulled, diesel-powered craft, the best of the war. They were good sea boats, and could really stand in for destroyer types.

The British had their motor torpedo boats (MTBs), planing-hulled, gasoline-powered 70-footers. With these, the Coastal Forces fought S-boats in the North Sea and English Channel, and in the Mediterranean. The gasoline was easily set on fire.

The United States had its patrol torpedo boats (PTs), similar to the British models, but adding radar. We employed some in the English Channel and the Mediterranean, but it was in the southwest Pacific that they proved of most value. There among the islands they fought deadly duels with Japanese destroyers, cut up their landing craft, sank transports and supply ships.

Russian torpedo cutters were designed from the original British coastal motor boats. These were light 63-footers with hydroplane hulls, gasoline-powered and very fast. They were widely used in the Baltic and Black Seas.

All these boats originally carried torpedoes as their primary armament, sometimes depth charges or mines, light automatic weapons, and smoke floats. They ferried raiding parties.

As the range, accuracy, and destructive power of relatively light, cheap, precision-guided munitions burgeoned in the postwar years, FACs came into their own. FACs play a major role in the narrow seas today. Coastal defense and escort of convoys calls for large numbers of high-speed craft in the 110- to 140-foot range, surface-oriented patrol boats capable of carrying not only torpedoes, depth charges, mines, and guns, but also guided missiles. Not all at once but in some combination, of course. These are lean, mean machines.

As requirements in terms of range and performance have inevitably (and inexorably) grown, boats have become as much as 50 feet longer. The larger have displacement hulls. As size has increased, so has versatility, stability, and seakeeping ability. Short range offensive-defense has given way to limited offense. AA and ASW are being added.

Missile-armed FACs have become low cost substitutes for the larger and generally slower combatants (destroyers, frigates, even corvettes) fewer and fewer can afford. While potent beyond their size, the operational tradeoff is still to some degree in seaworthiness and range. Electronics take up more and more of the weight and space allowance. Moreover, FACs tend to be designed closely to their intended use, with very little allowance for future needs. They are more easily replaced than they are updated.

Manned by many of a navy's natural fighters—they find their way to the FACs by one means or another, no matter what the rules—these boats operate as a rule by flotilla (squadron) (four to six boats) or half flotilla. They do not hesitate to take on major ships. They endlessly fight their own kind. They attack and defend mine craft. In particularly dangerous waters they escort convoys. They themselves lay mines. They raise havoc with coastal traffic, merchant and naval.

To give the flotillas maximum mobility, each can be based on a tender—typically a 3000-ton converted cargo ship. These tenders carry fuel, ammunition, food, and water. They can undertake major repairs. They carry the flotilla staff and furnish them with office space. They provide accommodation for the crews, and a target ship for practice runs.

Newer FACs can escort amphibious vessels across narrow seas such as the Baltic and Black Seas. They are the capital ships of the narrow seas.

Neutrals as well as client states have received large numbers of FACs, including all sizes. They all remain vulnerable to tactical air strike, and to be fully effective they must be furnished adequate air cover.

SUBMARINES

In the narrow seas, submarines typically are the smaller coastal (600–1300-ton) diesel electric–powered boats. Smaller submarines are better able to operate in the shallow water, reaching more places and disappearing more easily. Diesel submarines are quieter, and therefore harder to find. They are also easier to operate with an only semitrained crew. They are cheaper than nuclear-powered ones, and so do not completely drain a country's naval budget. There can be more of them. Range is not such a critical factor here, in any case. Guns and torpedoes remain the principal offensive armament here. Cruise missiles are being added.

The hulls of modern submarines are constructed of new high-tensile, nonmagnetic steel. They are capable of operating at depths of 660 feet. They will do 25 knots surfaced, and about the same submerged, for short sprints. They have a submerged endurance of six days while covering nearly 1000 miles at 6 knots, on the battery. They are being equipped to fire wire-guided torpedoes, and submarine-launched missiles. Fewer and fewer carry guns. Almost all can lay mines. Anechoic coatings make them difficult to detect.

Small diesels can attack and sink surface vessels, merchant and naval. They can mine limited areas. They can provide beach reconnaissance and land special operations forces. Satellites and inertial navigation systems give them precise positioning twenty-four hours a day. Communications via satellite are rapid, reliable, and secure. "Smart" missiles and torpedoes have ranges well beyond any target ship's detection range.

Submarines on operational patrols are generally confined to working against the approaches to naval ports and in confined waters in frequent use by the enemy. It is in these traffic focal and seaway choke points that enemy ship movements that obey the laws of probability produce the best targets. Here ships can be found, fixed, and then fought with the least expenditure of time and fuel.

For the future, Italy, West Germany, and Sweden have introduced the first modern closed-cycle submarine propulsion plants small enough for use as alternatives to diesel engines. The German version uses a hydrogen and oxygen fuel cell, the Swedish a Stirling engine. Canada is marketing a mini-nuclear plant, small enough to be just plugged in. These might not, however, be able to stand up to the wear and tear of Third World crews.

The Australian Navy includes small diesel submarines, for the reasons we have described. So do the navies of Japan, India, Turkey, and Cuba, among others. The number is growing slowly but surely every year.

MINES

The narrow seas are mine country. Mines are, in any case, the natural weapon of a small navy, especially a markedly inferior one. Mines have developed to a surprising sophistication; they are relatively cheap, easy to handle, and deadly. Mines can be employed defensively and/or offensively. Defensively, they can be used to deny large sea areas, preventing an enemy's approach, or passage. They can disrupt and delay. Offensively, they can be used to disorganize the enemy's maritime supply system; deny safe ports and secure shipping routes; sink and damage its ships; and impose an expensive countermine effort.

Mines—bottom, moored, or floating; contact, influence, or controlled—can be laid from almost any of the whole range of naval, merchant, and fishing platforms. These include surface ships, submarines, and aircraft.

Effectively, everyone has them or has access to them and will use them. They are a frequent gift to smaller allies or client states.

Moored contact mines—the original operational type—can weigh as much as 1000 pounds, a quarter of that consisting of explosive. They can easily be laid in waters up to 1000 feet deep. For them, cable weight is the limiting factor; too much cable will pull the mine down.

Bottom influence mines—essentially a WWII development—

can weigh half a ton, more than half of that explosive. They work best in waters with depths of 150 feet or less. Their sensor range limits them; in water deeper than that, activation influences do not penetrate strongly enough to activate the mine.

In both world wars, the overall mining pattern was the same. In WWI and again in WWII, almost all of these European mines were laid in the great arc of its bordering seas, waters stretching from the Baltic through the North Sea and the English Channel to the Mediterranean, Adriatic, and Black Seas. Narrow seas, all.[2]

Once planted in a target area, mines of all types remain an effective threat until swept, cleared individually, or after the legally required six months they self-sterilize. In practical terms, this means almost indefinitely, since this last cannot be depended on.

Although moored contact mines continue to be produced in large numbers, modern mines tend to be influence-activated bottom types. Ground mines are considerably more sophisticated, containing many more technical anti-sweeping devices. But also, ground mines tend to imbed themselves in the bottom where they lie. Their clearance can tax even the best mine-hunting units, especially when types are mixed. Although any field not covered by fire can sooner or later be swept, under war conditions a well designed minefield is substantially impossible to clear within any reasonable period of time.

Thus, any mine campaign based on sufficient numbers and types of mines has a high probability of success. Unless, that is, sufficient of the mine delivery platforms can be intercepted before reaching the target area.

Limpet mines present a special case of their own, being the archetypal weapon of unconventional warfare. Limpets are small, light, and extremely simple, making them the near-perfect weapon for frogmen. They can be set to explode at either a set time, or after the host ship has traveled a certain distance, or some combination of both. Just a few limpets properly and judiciously placed can create shipping chaos.

MINE COUNTERMEASURE SHIPS AND CRAFT

Any mine countermeasure effort must be seen as a whole. To be complete, it must include the demagnetizing (degaussing and deperming) of both merchant and naval vessels; the organization and training of a mine spotting and reporting system; and the organization, training and equipping of a minesweeping force. This effort can soak up a tremendous number of assets, all considered, in navies where these things are scarce.

Mine countermeasure ships and craft fall into three main categories: minesweepers, minehunters, and craft of opportunity. Minesweepers have been around as a type since WWI and the moored contact mine was recognized as a serious threat. Sweepers tend to deal with mines collectively, as fields. Minehunters are a post–WWII idea, dealing with bottom mines one by one. Craft of opportunity are auxiliary sweepers converted from civilian types.

Minesweepers—from 600-ton ships built to show a minimum magnetic signature down to 40-ton boats built for extremely shallow water—usually work in pairs, a moored-mine sweep cable streamed between them. Single ship sweeps are also common, however. As a rule, they are equipped to deal with all types of sweepable mines. Sweepers clear harbor entrances, their approaches offshore, and the critical sea lanes, cutting mines loose or purposely setting them off. They patrol friendly minefields and nets. They may on occasion even lay or relay a field or two.

Attrition rates among minesweepers are high. The mines themselves get many of them. The sweepers hit the very mines for which they are searching, either because one has escaped previous sweeps or because one has broken loose from its moor and is adrift. Or the sweepers—equipped primarily for contact sweeping—run into mixed fields and set off an influence mine. Minehunters pick up the pieces.

The sweepers also suffer continually and inescapably from air attack. Tied either to their sweep gear in the middle of a minefield or to a convoy, they are seldom free to maneuver. Their AA armament can never be sufficient to keep attacking planes at a safe distance, nor can enough ammunition for a long defense be carried on board.

Minehunters are similar, but instead of conventional sweep gear work with precise positioning equipment, side-scan radar, and robots, exploding or removing mines one by one, remotely. They work primarily in shallower water, ports, and their approaches.

Fishing trawlers, offshore oil service vessels, tugs, and other craft of opportunity can comparatively easily be converted to rudimentary minesweepers of one kind or another. Once mobilized, they carry out most preliminary and routine sweeping, only being supported as necessary by the always too few regulars.

AMPHIBIOUS CRAFT

Conventional landing craft typically are self-propelled barges of various sizes, measuring up to about 170 tons, capable of an average ten or so knots, of shallow draft, with wide, flat, open decks. The bigger ones can move three loaded trucks or 100 tons of mixed cargo, or some combination thereof. Being flat-bottomed, they can run right up to a beach, lower their bow ramps, and immediately handle cargo. They are widely used for routine logistics as well as assault.

The French Navy played a major supporting role in Indochina between 1945 and 1954, as France attempted to reassert its authority there. The navy furnished air and gunfire support, external administrative and internal combat transport, moving troops, guns, ammunition, and supplies. It executed a number of assault landings, starting with small-scale ones around Saigon in 1945 and the major one at Haiphong in 1946. Out of this developed the original and very effective *dinassauts*—naval infantry units of company and battalion size, complete with their own organic landing craft for command, reconnaissance, transport, and gunfire support—to fight the riverine war. Dinassauts were a permanent contribution to naval ideas.

For those who can assemble enough of them, helicopters offer a way around the limitations of conventional landing craft. In a vertical envelopment, helos are able to lift assaulting troops over a beach, placing them directly on top of the objective, and then supplying them. Few small navies possess much capability here. But small helo-borne raids are always a possible threat.

The development of amphibious air cushion vehicles (ACVs, or LCACs) provides another alternative. Out to a distance of approximately 200 miles, it is now possible for assault forces to move shore-to-shore, at speed. A 40-knot ACV-borne force can materially shorten both its assembly and transit times, and fall upon a hostile shore with little or no warning. It now has a choice of 70 percent of beaches. ACVs are armed with light self-defense weapons that can, if useful, give limited covering fire.

As the use of military force becomes more politically constrained, amphibious strikes can provide a discriminating use of force, with high impact for the use of relatively few assets. We shall see more of them, in whatever form. No matter how tricky they are.

OMAN

The Sultan of Oman's Navy represents an atypically strong, homogeneous, modern, professional Third World locally oriented fighting navy. Threatened at one time by invasion from South Yemen and by internal subversion and revolution in the name of Arab socialism, Oman bought itself a high tech force, paid for with oil. The navy is heavy on FACs and includes a relatively strong amphibious element. The total absence of any mine warfare craft should also be noted.

The Omani Navy's first priority must be defense of its coast, including the Strait of Hormuz's internationally strategic south shore. Its second involves some indeterminate reach beyond immediate control of coastal waters, designed within coalition (GCC[3]) needs. It operates the Strait of Hormuz VTS (vessel traffic system) (see Table 1).

Table 1
Sultan of Oman's Navy

Ships: 8 FACs (gun and missile armed)
            4 inshore patrol craft (gun armed)
            2 LSTs
            3 LCMs
            2 LCUs
            1 training ship (and 1 sail training ship)
            9 coastal patrol craft (Royal Oman Police)
Planes: 4 maritime patrol aircraft (on loan
            from Air Force)
Bases: 4 (Wudan - main base;
            Khor Muscat;
            al-Ghanam - in the Strait of Hormuz; Salalah)

A civilian water tanker is under charter, supplying villages without
adequate supplies of their own.

Source: P. Lewis Young, "The Sultan of Oman's Navy," *Navy International*
     (February 1989), pp. 53-58.

The navy is heavily larded with seconded and contract British officers, ensuring that atypically high standard of service.
These are, however, rapidly being phased out as the force ma-
tures and the Omanis become qualified to take over. Those in
key positions may nonetheless be around for a long time.

WEST GERMANY

West Germany—left after World War II with a small outlet
on the Baltic (Lübeck, Kiel, and the rest of the Schleswig-Hol-
stein coast) as well as all of Germany's prewar North Sea coast—
possesses one of the finer small Western European navies, a
true reflection of German technology. In these waters it inher-
its the traditional German naval role, a more than ever necessary one. Firmly committed to the Western democracies, Bonn

consciously decided right from the beginning (in 1955) to integrate its limited rearmament efforts with those of the North Atlantic Treaty Organization (NATO). It thereby also acquired treaty as well as national strategic interest in the Danish Straits.

Wilhelmshaven and Kiel were redesignated as the *Bundesmarine*'s main bases. To the organized civilian minesweeping cadres—and to a few civilianized S-boats (motor torpedo boats) similarly working (on Baltic surveillance tasks) for the British— were added five M-boats (minesweepers), war booty returned by France. Destroyers came from the United States, frigates (corvettes) from Britain, aircraft from both. A couple of the best of the scuttled U-boats were salvaged and refitted. The new fleet was on its way.

The *Bundesmarine* can be classified today as a regional navy-plus, with three priority tasks. Its first priority must be defense of German coastal lines of communication, protecting its small remaining outlet on the Baltic. Its second priority involves some reach beyond immediate coastal defense, designed within coalition warfare (NATO) needs. It would cooperate closely with Denmark in holding the straits. Last, it would contribute to NATO's other forces, as it can.

The *Bundesmarine* includes two squadrons of destroyers, and two of frigates, destined for the North Sea. There are four squadrons of S-boats, for the Danish Straits and the Baltic. There are two squadrons of submarines. Minesweepers are organized into six squadrons, forming the largest single element. The land-based naval air arm counts a reconnaissance fighter squadron, three fighter-bomber squadrons, and two maritime patrol squadrons. It forms a worthy successor to those which have gone before.[4]

NOTES

1. Strip alert: aircraft are on the ground, fully serviced and armed, at the end of the runway, ready to take off.

2. Ellis A. Johnson and David A. Katcher, *Mines Against Japan* (White Oak, MD: Naval Ordnance Laboratory, 1973), pp. 2–5. Gregory K. Hartmann, *Weapons That Wait* (Annapolis, MD: Naval Institute Press, 1979), p. 71.

3. Gulf Cooperation Council: Oman, Saudi Arabia, the United Arab Emirates, Qatar, Bahrain, and Kuwait.

4. Militärgeschichtlichen Forschungsamt, *30 Jahre Bundeswehr 1955–1985* (Mainz, v.Hase & Koehler, 1985), pp. 155–70.

2

Coast Guards

What is a coast guard? What are—or should be—its legal functions? The world is full of maritime armed forces—all really quasi navies—performing various recognized coast guard functions. The models supplied by the larger naval powers, however, are so dissimilar as to offer little real guidance to others; they serve to make definition of tasks and functions much less clear than might otherwise be.

Basic to any coast guard is the concept that it is composed of three major elements: the *national headquarters*, responsible for policies and plans and for overall supervision of the service; the *operating units* like the larger ships (cruising cutters), if any, the more numerous smaller patrol boats, and the aircraft (fixed and rotary wing); and the various *shore facilities* such as surface bases, air stations, shipyards, depots, and schools. Emphasis between these elements can and does vary between forces, depending upon their perceived tasks.

The Russian version of a coast guard (the Maritime Border Guard) is apparently a large, simple police force carrying internal physical security to the extreme. The British Coastguard is essentially a small coast watcher unit, slowly acquiring additional coordination responsibilities, especially in search and rescue. The Russian is a military force, the British is not.

The 44,600-man strong U.S. Coast Guard—some 39,000 uniformed personnel plus 5,600 civil service civilians, forming probably the tenth largest navy in the world—performs everything the British Coastguard does, as well as all that Trinity House and the RNLI do. It also does fisheries protection, marine inspection, customs and immigration, and more. It can fight—if it has to.

First developed in 1790 as the Revenue Cutter Service (to collect Treasury Secretary Hamilton's new duties), the U.S. Coast Guard will be offered here as the model of a fully developed, cost-effective coast guard force. It is a military service.

Recall the role played by the United States' tiny naval and revenue cutter "mosquito fleet" in the Floridas during the Seminole Wars (1834–42), for instance. Or by the coast guard's predecessors in Alaska from its earliest days as a territory, when first revenue cutter *Lincoln* (1867), then *Bear*, and then others policed the wild and icebound coast; administered law where there was none; rescued whalers; protected seals; fed the starving; and succored the lost, sick, stranded, and hurt. Or by the Coast Guard during Prohibition's "rum wars" (1920–34) or today's "drug war." It is by such means that the state's writ is made to run.

The larger part of the world—the Third World's new maritime states—are still struggling to sort all this out. On their answers depends the organization of a significant part of their government, the allocation of usually very scarce men and money, and the purchase of costly materiel. This is, therefore, a major issue for these states and the one we shall discuss here.

THE THREE TASKS

Any fully developed coast guard's missions and tasks could be formally divided into four major groups: maritime law enforcement, marine safety, marine pollution control, and maritime defense. In the United States, they are.

The maritime law enforcement role breaks down into interdiction of smugglers, interdiction of illegal aliens, EEZ (fisheries) enforcement, and a wide assortment of minor other items. This directly reflects its status as the federal maritime police force. It includes today's drug war, an activity which soaks up a quarter of its total effort.

The maintenance of good order in the territorial seas and to a lesser extent in the EEZ is for the coastal state a responsibility as much as a right. Resource enjoyment calls for the exclusion of those not entitled, for environmental protection, and for the proper exercise of right by those entitled to do so.

Also primary, marine safety translates into search and rescue, merchant marine/boating safety, aids to navigation, port safety, and leads into pollution control.

Maritime defense is only contributory, but with us includes administration of the maritime defense zones, port security, naval control of shipping, inshore patrol, and convoy escort, as well as operational control of various navy inshore warfare units. More on these as we go.

SHIPS AND CRAFT

To meet coast guard functions, fast powerfully armed *gunboats* are not called for. The object is not ever to kill the maximum number of people, in the shortest possible time, in the cheapest way. Rather, the opposite is the case. Gunboats today are in any case also too expensive to buy, to man, and to run. They are, in addition, less than optimized to carry out coast guard functions.

The U.S. Coast Guard's normal operations areas are our ports, inland waterways, territorial sea, and 200-mile fisheries conservation zone. This is a relatively low-threat environment that generally matches the defensive capabilities of most of the 240 Coast Guard surface platforms 65-feet or over.[1] The same should be true of most other operating areas.

What may be needed are *cruising cutters* (roughly corvettes), large (up to 2000 tons) for their type, sea kindly (habitable for long periods), economical to run, of moderate speed—exceptionally reliable ships. They must be strong and easy to maintain; capable of search and rescue, towing, fighting fires, and rudimentary pollution control/salvage work—a good stable platform from which to operate boarding parties. Twenty-six knots would be speed enough (the on board helicopters do the high-speed chases).

These cutters must have a helicopter pad, and carry a helo to give them true reach and speed of response. They require armament sufficient only for police actions—perhaps a small (3-inch?) gun and a pair of light (20-mm or 50-cal) automatic weapons. Always they must be easily identifiable as coast guard (distinctive ensign, police blue light, unique livery, etc.). They should naturally be cheaper than dedicated men o'war. Any war-fighting capability must fall out naturally from this. Here the Royal Navy's *Castle* class offshore patrol vessels provide an excellent model. The *Castles* did yeoman work in the Falklands (1982).

"Public service" functions represent roughly 15 percent of the total activity of the French Navy. Six out of twelve newly programmed 2600-ton frigates will be stripped down versions called *frégates de surveillance*. They will in fact be the coast guard cruising cutters we have talked about. Norway uses the same kind of cutter.

These large cruising cutters are used for the more difficult distant patrols, lasting for up to a month at a time. These cutters are *not* cost-effective when used for most closer, shorter tasks. Something else is required for that. Search and rescue might be the exception, of course.

Needed also are *offshore patrol boats*, 110–125-feet in size, to cover those nearer waters. Most services require more of these. They too should be sea kindly, economical cruisers, but in this case capable of bursts of speed. They too should provide a stable platform for coast guard work, normally capable of patrols of up to a week. One wicked-looking 20-mm and two 30-cal machine guns are more than sufficient weaponry. Distinctive flag, light, and livery remain a must.

Needed, too, are numbers of harbor craft (police boats); a tug or two, perhaps; lifeboats, buoy tenders, sometimes landing craft; and occasionally even such things as a small water tanker or cargo ship. All must also be easily identified as coast guard, a police presence at all times.

Aircraft—shore-based or shipborne—can also play major coast guard roles for such tasks as sovereignty patrols, surveillance, pollution control, search and rescue, underway replenishment, and chase. The U.S. Coast Guard operates some 220 fully integrated (organic) fixed and rotary-wing planes, each one materially extending the reach and speed of response of our various shore and afloat units. Our task would be impossible without them.

Not every small military-maritime force can boast an organic air arm, however, as badly as they are needed. For some, there is just not the money. For others, interservice rivalry gets in the way. In some instances, both reasons may exist. Any country is the poorer for this omission, no matter why.

IMPOSING THE LAW

Complete overlapping surveillance of any of the frontier zones where there is a potential waterbone threat to law and order is in any case a first necessity for any force. This means surface and air patrols, radar, and where available, satellite. Only when one knows what is actually going on offshore can measures to assert control rationally be developed.

The coast guard has developed the use of aerostats, unmanned helium-filled balloons mounting a large radar. Based on modified 200-foot-by-50-foot offshore supply-type vessels, each tethered balloon rides as high as 2500 feet. These aerostats are used to monitor the sea surface and the air above. They detect unidentified—and therefore suspicious—surface vessels and low-flying aircraft, "skunks" that could be carrying illegal cargo such as people or drugs. They are useful for search and rescue, too.

The coastal surveillance organization, properly so-called, thus gives warning of not only navigational problems but also of unauthorized violations of the territorial sea, or of the economic or maritime defense zones, coming from either direction—outside or in. It then identifies an actual intruder from among the other shipping likely to be present. It vectors surface or air interception units to the target, supervises the investigation, and determines final disposition of the "skunk." This ideal is seldom wholly met at this level of naval development, however. Most small navies can carry out only spotty surveillance, and therefore exercise less than complete control.

The RN's Fishery Protection Squadron oversees fishing activity around United Kingdom coasts and surveils Britain's extensive offshore oil installations. It provides another good example of what a navy can do, if it will. Its experience is that mere RN presence is enough to result in compliance with the law. Nightstick-happy policing plays no part in their activities. Armament can be as little as a light automatic gun and a number of individual weapons.

RN boarding parties are traditionally unarmed, save in the most exceptional circumstances, however. USCG boarding parties, on the other hand, regularly carry sidearms, sometimes other weapons (rifles, shotguns), as considered prudent, and occasionally wear bulletproof vests.

Enforcement of international conventions is a frequent operational problem for a coast guard. Interpretation of their provisions is usually a complicated matter. States sign one treaty but not another. Those that sign often take reservations. Some sign none, and are bound by none. Patrolling cutters must determine whether a violation has in fact taken place, and then collect proper and sufficient evidence to report it to the flag state.

In peacetime, moreover, boarding a foreign flag ship on the high seas beyond the EEZ or within another's waters requires permission of the flag or host state.[2] This involves a cutter's report of the suspected delict to base, a request to headquarters, contacting the embassy for permission, then transmitting this back down the chain to the waiting cutter. By this time, it is often too late to prevent the suspect's escape. Not always, however.

First of all a maritime police force, the U.S. Coast Guard is today extensively engaged in just such police work, activity which harkens back to its Prohibition rum war of the 1920s. Today we have the drug war.

In September 1989, in a single night in two different marine operations, the United States seized more than 2700 pounds of cocaine, a 236-foot coastal freighter, 42-foot fishing boat, and three speedboats—and arrested nineteen people.

In the first of these two operations, Vanuatu-flagged coastal freighter *Nerma* and three smuggler's speedboats were seized by the U.S. Coast Guard off Burrows Cay in the Bahamas, along with 1100 pounds of cocaine. Seven of the freighter's Danish crew were held, as were the six people aboard the three boats waiting nearby to make the final cargo dash ashore.

Burrows was an apparently unpopulated cay, lying within waters the U.S. Coast Guard had standing Bahamian permission to patrol. There may have even been a Bahama police representative on board one of the cutters.

Nerma had been video-taped lying off Burrows Cay and visually observed off-loading obvious drugs. A statement of no objection having been obtained from Vanuatu (which had no record of her), the vessel was boarded and seized by *Manitou*, a 110-foot U.S. Coast Guard cutter. *Nerma* was escorted to Coast Guard Base Miami Beach for a dockside search, and more cocaine was found. The freighter and crew were held for conspiracy to import narcotics.

One of the three speedboats was seized after it was seen leaving Burrows Cay at high speed, the two people on board throwing bales and barrels over the side. It took another 110-footer—USCGC *Maui*—several warning bursts of light automatic fire to stop it.

About three hours later, two more speedboats were seen leaving Burrows Cay. One was caught by *Maui* and taken in. After a dockside boarding found evidence of cocaine, its two-man crew was arrested and the boat seized for conspiracy to import. The last boat was caught by 110-foot USCGC *Farallon* after a chase, the boat and its crew arrested after another successful dockside search, using dogs.

In the second of the two operations, federal agents also seized the fishing boat and 1600 pounds of cocaine. Six crewmen were arrested in this one. It had been a busy night.

PORT SAFETY AND SECURITY

Now to a basic player in coast guard operations. The U.S. Coast Guard provides a captain of the port (COTP) for every port in the United States. His territory extends to nearby secondary ports, his authority out to sea to the extent of U.S. jurisdiction there. No part of the coast is beyond the purview of one COTP or another. The COTPs are visible evidence of the federal presence on every side and of its concern for maritime safety and marine law enforcement.

The COTP will have one or more operating bases under his command. There are stationed most of his operational assets—patrol boats, tugs, and the like. There he will be host to tenant units—large cruising cutters, buoy tenders—under the operational control of higher levels—district or area. Lifeboat stations will, of course, be scattered to where needed. So will marine safety detachments, ashore.

Within his area, the COTP is responsible for the operational safety and security of the port, the ships that use it, the offshore structures, and the surrounding population, insofar as federal laws and Coast Guard regulations affect them. In this the COTP will cooperate with a variety of other agencies but the responsibility is his. He is the one who regulates. He inspects. He responds to emergencies, including search and rescue. For most marine accidents, it is he who coordinates the overall federal effort.

The COTP has authority commensurate with his wide-ranging responsibility. He may inspect every ship entering his port area, to ascertain compliance with regulations. Almost every tank vessel is inspected. So are many of the other ships. If he has reason to suspect violations, he may refuse a ship permission to enter until they are corrected or the misunderstanding is cleared up. He monitors its stay, including keeping an eye on cargo operations. He must concur in clearance of the ship.

To assist the COTP in his work the coast guard maintains a central master computer file containing the past condition and behavior history of all ships using U.S. ports. Each COTP has access to this file through a computer terminal. By this means he obtains a "dump" of the record on every ship due to arrive in his area (by law, twenty-four-hour notice of arrival must be given). It is by this means that the priority of inspection is established, determined through some combination of past behavior and time since last visit by the CG. Personnel are not unlimited. The COTP updates the file when the subject ship leaves.

Working with the COTP usually is an OCMI (officer-in-charge, marine inspection), responsible specifically for the more technical aspects of merchant marine safety. It is the OCMI who carries out the periodic technical inspections of vessels and licenses merchant personnel. It is he who investigates accidents. Not every small coast guard will both want and be able to man such an OCMI (more on this below).

In many U.S. ports, the COTP has absorbed the OCMI, the COTP now wearing "two hats" as the new MSO (marine safety officer). The MSO is only an administrative convenience, allowing better management of all personnel available in a given area, and will be more and more the case.

PIRACY

Piracy has been reborn and is a continuing law and order problem worldwide. Piracy can be defined as any armed violence at sea that is not a lawful act of war. It is any illegal (customarily prohibited) act of violence or detention committed at sea. It is terrorism at sea. Piracy—either state-sponsored or private—is endemic to many of the narrow seas. It seems to go hand in hand with smuggling, illegal immigration, slaving, and gun running, all of which thrive today.

Up to the nineteenth century, maritime terrorism was an almost universal curse. In those days, maritime terrorism most often took the form of piracy, which even in Britain was a recognized tool of state. Unofficially condoned, it was utilized to weaken an opponent's economic life, and add to one's own coffers. Navies began that way.

In 1775 a party of Maine woodsmen used an unarmed lumber schooner to surprise and capture a fully armed British warship off the coast of Machias, Maine. Guns and ammunition taken from that ship were used to bring in yet other British ships as prizes. These actions—executed by ordinary citizens without commissions, letters of marque, or legal authority of any sort (piracy, of course)—opened the proud history of the U.S. Navy. The navy was officially born by order of the Continental Congress only later that year.

The civilized nations of the world succeeded in putting piracy down during the mid-1800s. It was getting in the way of their burgeoning trade. Piracy has only recently experienced a resurgence.

It has still often been risky for Western merchantmen to pass too close to North Africa's Barbary Coast or the Persian Gulf's Trucial Coast. Steaming the Straits of Malacca or the South China Sea long invited Malay, Moro, or Chinese pirates, coming up over the rail with kris, bolo, or gun. The Caribbean was notoriously unsafe even for convoyed merchantmen until the United States hanged forty of them in New Orleans, in 1850. That discouraged most of the others.

But after WWII, a number of Third World governments—old and new—rediscovered the thought that terrorist tactics, even at sea, carried out either directly or by proxy, were in some cases a seemingly useful means of gaining political ends. We began to see the reemergence of protected—if unacknowledged—piracy which soon became terrorism on a global scale. Private entrepreneurs, recognizing a good thing when they saw one, in many cases joined in.

The breaking of the old peace-keeping empires has hastened this process. Under Pax Britannica the world's sea lanes were kept secure for trade—theirs and anyone else's not a threat. The pax is now gone. The proliferation of small new states—many incapable of adequately policing their own waters, or uninterested in doing so—just adds to the problem, especially when these states claim extensive territorial seas.

On January 22, 1961, *Santa Maria*, a 21,500-ton 20-knot Portuguese flag cruise liner, was hijacked off Curaçao (Netherlands Antilles) by a group of Portuguese revolutionaries. The crew was Portuguese, the passengers mixed, including some U.S. citizens. Several of the crew were shot, one died.

For eleven days *Santa Maria* cruised the crowded Caribbean

and the nearby Atlantic, right in our own back yard, so to speak. The United States alone committed eighteen planes, four destroyers, and two oilers to the task of finding her, yet took three days to do so. The Portuguese (naturally), British, Dutch, and Spanish also had forces on the trail. Still, it was late on the twenty-fifth before it was located and tracking began.

Intensive negotiations followed. In the end, *Santa Maria* was voluntarily surrendered off Recife (Brazil), February 2, to the Brazilian Navy. It was twelve days later. The point had been made.

Today neither the Mediterranean nor the Caribbean are secure from this scourge. The Caribbean saw the seizure of *Santa Maria*, and still sees the steady disappearance of private yachts without a trace. The Mediterranean saw the seizure of *Achille Lauro* (1985), and the murder of one of its passengers.

In October 1985, *Achille Lauro*, a Greek flag cruise liner steaming the eastern Mediterranean, was seized by Arab terrorists. Its passenger list included a number of Americans, one of whom (aged, sick, confined to a wheelchair) was executed and his body dumped into the sea. Egypt finally granted the Arabs asylum, but flew them right out. Their plane was tracked and forced down in Sicily by U.S. naval aircraft. The terrorists were seized by the Italians; most were tried and sentenced to prison.

The Straits of Malacca and the South China Sea remain dangerous today. U.S. flag *Mayaguez* was seized in the South China Sea off Cambodia, in 1975, in a brazen act of governmental piracy. We shall come back to this in a little bit.

Merchantmen at anchor in Manila Bay are boarded and the ships looted. In one case, a master was shot on his own bridge.

But the most violent attacks take place around the Indonesian coast, most affecting local craft. During one incident, passengers and crew were lined up. Ten were shot dead; the remainder jumped overboard; 25 of them drowned.

Next must come the Gulf of Siam, where "innocent" fishermen regularly board Vietnamese refugee boats, looting, raping, and murdering. Two Thai fishing boats raided a Vietnamese refugee boat in June 1989, and perhaps 150 refugees were lost. This, too, is treated as a local police problem, ignored by most.

Singapore Strait, one of the busiest waterways in the world, currently sees the blatant pirating of a merchant ship on the average of every two to four days. These pirates even attack ships underway at sixteen knots, coming alongside from astern, boarding with the aid of grappling irons and climbing ropes or poles.

During daylight hours, Singapore Strait is patroled by the light naval forces of the three riparian states—Singapore, Malaysia, and Indonesia. At dark this protection had disappeared. Singapore's port authority was concerned but apparently powerless. The police reportedly held that pirates were a matter for the navy, and that they had no jurisdiction outside port limits anyway. The navy claims it was fully occupied with defense of the island, and that law and order is strictly the concern of the police. So it goes.

Singapore Strait is a difficult body of water to negotiate even when conditions are favorable. Piracy only adds to the passage difficulties, increasing the risk of collision, ramming, or grounding; death or injury; damage or loss of cargo; and environmental pollution.

SECURITY OF MERCHANT ASSETS

International law, as still systematized and codified, states that on the high seas, or outside the jurisdiction of any state, the pirate is *hostis humani generis*, an outlaw. The agent of any state may seize him; the courts of any state may try him. It does not matter that the pirate flies the flag of another state, or claims its citizenship. Legally, he is everyone's enemy.

Not so, however, in anything considered the territorial sea. There, only the coastal state has jurisdiction over him, and jealously guards this right. The potential rescuing patrol boat of another state, if it takes action against a pirate in such waters, runs the risk of being accused at the very least of non-innocent passage, probably of intrusion or intervention, perhaps even of a hostile act. Piracy is most effectively attacked at its bases. Today these are all effectively protected under some flag or another, usually beyond reach of those who would police them.

Port congestion is epidemic throughout the developing world, providing one of the best environments for both official and unofficial piracy. Congested ports mean that merchantmen have to queue for berths for long periods out in the roads, protected in terms of weather but not of safety for ship, crew, passengers, or cargo. Berthing pierside seldom improves the security situation. Along the seething Third World waterfronts, vessels are often fair game.

Shoreside piers, cargo areas, and oil terminals are at least as vulnerable. Although they usually enjoy somewhat better physical security, they remain easily got at by determined raiders.

Offshore oil and gas exploration and production structures enjoy no better security than ships. Operating in an even more remote and hostile environment, these rigs offer higher stakes, and are usually farther from help. The relative ease with which pirates can attack offshore facilities makes them especially inviting targets.

Port authorities and local police are too often found to be scarce, especially when most needed. Even when available, they are too frequently uninterested, subject to bribery, and in any case underarmed and undertrained for their job.

Blackmail is always possible. A well placed explosive charge or guided missile could seriously damage any such asset. Determined raiders could capture a rig, hold the crew hostage, or threaten to blow up the rig, thus causing a major oil spill or gas fire, unless their demands were met.

The waters of the narrow seas and the ports bordering them thus contain many assets with economic or symbolic value that are well within the capabilities of pirates. Prevention here, too, is better than response. The security task is not a part-time one. Politics not infrequently complicates it.

Even on the high seas, the problem of unilateral law enforcement may become more acute as time goes on. The number of naval vessels and planes available for this duty is markedly lower than in previous times. Think of the hunt in the Caribbean for *Santa Maria*, where it took three days just to find her. Moreover, navies are all the more hesitant to take action against suspects because of the almost inevitable politicization of anything—including self-defense—they as outsiders get into.

Neutralizing or, failing that, reacting to these threats will have to involve action by a coast guard at multiple levels, to meet as many facets of the particular threat as can be under the circumstances given. As far as the coast guard is concerned, the countereffort begins with identification of the threat, that is, with adequate, accurate, and timely intelligence, presented to operating units in a form that they can use.

Good intelligence gives early warning of trouble and allows efficient allocation of whatever defensive resources are available to meet it. Without good intelligence, a truly meaningful response will be beyond the capability of whatever military-maritime means are likely to be available.

In any case, a coast guard can only orchestrate what must inevitably be a complicated military-maritime response. Involved must be the coast guard itself, of course; the local navy, if any; the ships and rigs themselves; the owners, and the port, with its police and fire units—all these, along with whatever outside help shows up.

HURRICANE HUGO

The U.S. Virgin Islands—St. Thomas, St. John, and St. Croix— lie some 40 miles just to the east of Puerto Rico. St. Croix, about 40 miles to the south of St. Thomas, at 84 square miles, is considerably the largest of the three, and off by itself. Its people number 52,400, with Christiansted and Fredriksted their principal towns. There is a coast guard marine safety detachment stationed at the former.

In September 1989, a 140-mile-an-hour killer hurricane (Hugo) struck the islands, particularly St. Croix. It hit on a Monday, early. On Tuesday, two coast guard cutters—USCGCs *Bear* (a 270-footer) and *Vashon* (a 110-footer)—arrived at Christiansted, the first outsiders to appear there after the storm. They put ashore small landing parties to assess damage, see what could be done immediately to help, and temporarily to pull off the island's marine safety people. The landing parties found the island devastated, but this they expected. What they did not expect was the public services gone, the citizenry looting everything they could carry off, and government in a state of anarchy. Withdrawing in the face of *force majeure*, the men returned to their ships and called for more help. The first alarm was thereby sounded.

On Wednesday, two people swam out to *Vashon*—800 yards offshore—in fear of the mobs. After they had told their story, the coast guard sent armed landing parties back ashore and brought off more than 139 other people looking for safety from the looting and gunfire.

On Wednesday, several larger landing parties were put ashore at Fredriksted by two 110s. The coast guard continued to report and assisted in the restoration of order. The guard carried out search and rescue around and off the coast. It coordinated the combined military and civilian evacuation of the seriously injured and those tourists wishing to leave the island. Some six of its own cutters and several air units participated in the effort. The guard also responded to two oil spills.

In the end, it took 1100 troops and other federal agents to restore law and order fully to the island. They eventually left, their work done. The coast guard is always there.

The guard's activities during Hugo are typical of the public service aspect of its job. The guard performs this function in the loneliest islands and up the longest rivers, on all U.S. navigable waters.

READINESS AND RESERVE

As one of the United States' armed services, the coast guard falls under the jurisdiction of the navy in time of war or other national maritime emergency. As such, it forms a de facto naval reserve. Some coast guard tasks continue in time of war (buoy and light tending), some are even enlarged (port safety), some are dropped (recreational boating safety), and some new ones are added (control of shipping). Personnel are reassigned to reflect this.

The guard's cruising cutters—roughly equivalent to large underarmed corvettes—would in time of war receive their additional armament. They would mount surface-to-surface missiles (Harpoon?), some sort of close-in weapon system (Phalanx?), ASW torpedoes, and depth charges. They would exchange their normal on-board helo for an ASW-capable one (LAMPS?). The hull-mounted and towed sonars would be installed and put to work.

Smaller ships and craft would add proportionate armament, as needed. Most of this equipment is purchased and ready, stowed at various guard and navy bases. About one week's yard availability per ship would be required to get them ready. Augmenting personnel would join at that time, running short refresher courses as they do. Aviation units would undergo parallel reorientation for war.

In the United States, the guard is responsible to the navy for the maritime defense zones (MDZs). Reaching out 200 miles, there is one for each coast, replacing the navy's former sea frontier. To be activated in time of war or other emergency, the MDZ assumes control of all inshore warfare assets—including those belonging to the navy—joining them to their own to ensure port safety and security, coastal escort and patrol, minesweeping, naval control of shipping, and the like.

The guard itself has a reserve of some 12,000 officers and men largely devoted to port security, MSO, and shore staff augmentation. These reserves are targeted against specific wartime jobs, and drill with that in mind. They also provide a surge capability in time of peace, frequently serving extended active duty in their specialties.

In countries where there is no navy, but only a coast guard, the coast guard would carry out the same general preparations for war. In some cases, their normal operational environment is such that shifting to an overt war-fighting posture would result in little change, if any. Nonetheless, organization and training, plans and equipment must allow for adequate combat readiness *before* it is needed.

COSTA RICA

Costa Rica well represents with its new coast guard the lowest end of the naval spectrum discussed here. A normally quiet, developing Central American state, it provides a model of its kind. Costa Rica faces both a narrow sea—the Caribbean—and the Pacific. Unfortunately for it in 1989, it also shares borders with Panama to its south and Nicaragua to its north, both highly unstable, if for different reasons.

Starting with a nondescript prior maritime force, Costa Rica has begun to build a real coast guard as a visible and tangible symbol of sovereignty along its coasts and rivers, enforcing its laws and providing community support. It has a U.S. Coast Guard adviser.

The 130-man strong Costa Rican Coast Guard currently operates eight patrol boats from 36 feet to 105 feet in length, and thirteen Boston Whalers. There are bases on both coasts. There is no organic air element, but outside helicopters and light aircraft cooperating as needed greatly expand its capabilities. The coast guard earns its pay. A formal reserve is planned, so successful is it.

Costa Rica now has the capability to interdict drug trafficking through its waters, patrol its extensive fishing zones, and conduct search and rescue. The coast guard is even capable of a limited coastal defense. It works at it all.

Territorial defense is a primary mission, especially important because of its neighbors. The coast guard is directly responsible for the northern coasts and the river border. Search and rescue is also a first-level task, because of the large numbers of marginally equipped fishing boats working both coasts. Maritime law enforcement is a major continuing role. Costa Rica jealously guards its fisheries, and licenses are a must. Not least, the coast guard serves the coastal villages any way it can, occasionally even delivering babies.[3]

All beginning navies and all of the smallest ones should look like this. The public service function commences as soon as a military-maritime force is organized and continues throughout its existence, or until this function is sometime later broken off from a growing navy and turned over to a specialized coast guard.

These quasi navies have to be counted, too.

CAPABILITIES

Military capabilities include a measure of the whole range of things of significance of which a navy may in fact be capable— not what it will do but what it can do—given the forces at its disposal, the area(s) in which it must operate, and the opposition it must face. Its organization, the quality and quantity of its materiel, the skill and morale of its personnel, and the intelligence it has available are all factors in this calculus. Indicated at the same time are vulnerabilities.

Small navies may be categorized by comparing their military capabilities to their assigned missions and the supporting tasks, roughly as follows:

- Fair to excellent general purpose navies, limited principally by active strength and mobilization potential;
- Navies that are fair to excellent in one or two special types of operations (i.e., in minesweeping or ASW) at the expense of other possible types of operations. These usually are members of larger mutual defense forces, contributing specialized know-how along with available strength;
- Ineffective general purpose navies, more for show than for action; and
- Navies that are only (and are really intended only as) de facto coast guards, maritime safety, customs, or police forces.

As can easily be seen, technologically oriented military-maritime forces are less susceptible to being used for domestic political purposes than, say, ground forces. But any navy could become involved in nation-building activity. This role most often appears in, and greatly increases the manpower heaviness of the developing navies.

There is yet another significant dimension to a maritime force's possible internal roles: its potential as a countervailing political weight. In combination with an air force and the constabulary and/or police, small and weak though they may be, a coast guard can help counter the domination of a government by an overstrong army. In the developing societies, the established institutions of government are fragile at best. The distribution of armed power must often be carefully calculated, and a navy is sometimes created to help maintain internal balance.

Collateral capabilities for almost any service are activities related to exploration, hydrography, general oceanography, and environmental protection. These provide a useful and respected—even popular—peacetime role, as necessary in some places today as ever. These activities also often have political overtones, internationally as well as domestically.

NOTES

1. In 1989 there were 2200 ships and boats, in all.

2. This is true unless, on the high seas, continuous hot pursuit can be proven.

3. Phillip J. Heyl. "Costa Rica's Emerging Coast Guard," *U.S. Naval Institute Proceedings* (April 1989): 113–16.

3

War Fighting at Sea

COMMAND OF THE SEA

Command of the sea must be the ultimate aim of any navy. *Command* is the ability to use the sea for one's own purposes and at the same time deny this to an enemy. Command must be gained, maintained, and exploited. Each of these tasks demands a quite different mix of ships, planes, and craft, as we shall see. In peace or war.

Gaining command of the sea requires larger assembled or at least assemblable numbers of major combatants (ships and planes) with greater firepower and sea–keeping ability, forming a balanced fleet superior to that of the enemy. To secure command, this fleet must first of all maneuver so as to force the enemy into a decisive battle. In this, the major combatants of both sides go for broke, staking everything on one great effort.

Evidently, a weaker enemy was not apt to go for this. In that case, the weaker is driven from the sea and blockaded in port. From there he defends the coast and raids. He escorts coastal shipping, insofar as he is able. He waits, hoping to catch a part of the enemy force off guard and destroy it, thereby lessening the odds against him.

Historically, it has been shown that the naval defense of any coast best begins at the nearest enemy ports. Defense by means of offense—striking the enemy in his home bases before he can reach your own—became a key principle of British naval policy during the many Dutch, Spanish, and French wars. It remains valid today, open to any able force.

Maintaining command of the sea calls for a shift in the balance of the fleet: major combatants, yes, but a smaller number should suffice as long as they are fast; and a proportionately much larger number of escorts, minesweepers, patrol craft, and other "dust of the sea." It may also call for a special blockading force.

To continue to dispute command means keeping the weaker fleet in being, maintaining the threat, ready to exploit any mistakes on the part of the other. Minor sorties continue, keeping the weaker fleet tuned up and, hopefully, the stronger off balance.

Exploiting command of the sea requires sufficient troop and cargo transports, oilers, an amphibious force, escorts ready to utilize their now protected sea lanes (sea lines of communication (SLOCs)) to advantage. There must also be an adequate merchant and fishing fleet, furnishing auxiliaries to the navy, supporting the navy, and maintaining the civilian economy.

While these statements apply most easily to a super-navy, the principles involved apply even to a coast guard temporarily engaged in fighting a war. While the hardware may be scaled down, the rules stand as they are, even if they are sometimes harder to see.

It should be noted that command of the sea has two sides: a positive (one's own) and a negative (the foe's). Without control of both there is no command of the sea. Conversely, the proper application of the right tools, whether above, on, or below the surface—whatever tools—leading to command, results in seapower. Some measure of power, in any event.

Ideally, seapower is a flexible, general-purpose capability. It responds to the widest range of contingencies, and is not limited strictly to execution of a fixed list of predetermined tasks.

Such a list is always one task short, that being the one at hand. Among small navies, only a good regional navy can afford such a traditional balanced fleet. Smaller navies—stretched too thin—do not enjoy this option. They are rather forced to eliminate the peripheral tasks, building what is for them a flexible core force, without luxuries.

This book, therefore, has dealt and will continue to deal with command of the sea, not really with navies or air forces, per se. It is strategic folly to separate artificially the surface and air elements required to exercise command. Operational control—if nothing else—of these tools must rest in the hands of the navy. They are the sea warfare specialists.

BLOCKADE

Blockade is the use of naval forces to cut off maritime communications and supply. Blockades can be specialized. They can be classified into naval blockades, limited to preventing only the movement of specific military forces; and commercial blockades, stopping trade. Or they can be general, cutting off all seaborne movement, completely closing down a country's ports.

Blockade may be used to prevent the movement of contraband goods to an opponent's ports, or to him through a neutral. This is its most usual form.

In law, a list of specific goods considered contraband must be established, published, and made available to all. A blockade line must be set up. Shipping intelligence is provided the blockaders. Visit and search enforce the contraband rules.

Blockade may be just intended only to coerce an opponent into taking or refraining from some action or other. Blockade—although an undoubted act of war—may even be employed directly only to reinforce diplomacy, short of war. It is a most flexible instrument of government policy, frequently seen at this force intensity level.

As early as World War I, the submarine and the mine had begun to make a traditional close and continuous blockade too expensive a proposition for any fleet. Even then, the British clamped down on Germany, not off its North Sea ports as foreseen in prewar planning, but only at a distance. Blockade was exercised by forces stationed at the North Sea's western entrances, at the Orkneys in the north, and at Dover in the south.

Add now the FAC and the plane. Close and continuous blockade is not any longer possible except in the rarest of instances. Distant blockade is today the de facto norm, legal in traditional terms or not.

The United States has had considerable experience with blockade. In 1962, for instance, we found that without warning, the Soviet Union had brought some forty intermediate range ballistic missiles to Castro's Cuba. Our reconnaissance planes photographed them being set up. Reloads were following them in. A Soviet military advisory group accompanied them, to instruct the Cubans in their use and to help with the work. This gave the Soviets a major offensive capability for the first time to oppose the United States, using Cuba as its platform, bypassing our northern north-facing defenses. President Kennedy was furious.

For thirteen days, the United States played nuclear poker with Russia. Since the United States easily dominated the whole Caribbean area militarily, it was finally decided to declare a "quarantine" of Cuba, keeping open our other options while demonstrating that measures more violent were possible. All shipments of offensive weapons to Cuba were embargoed, and a blockade imposed to enforce this.

Backed by four of our aircraft carriers, a nineteen-ship blockade line was set up—thirteen destroyers supported by two cruisers and their escorts. The line was formed in a great arc extending 500 miles out to sea from Cape Maysi, Cuba's easternmost tip, across the principal sea routes into the island. Castro exploded. But although the Soviet Union had several submarines in the area, it lacked sufficient seapower to break the blockade.

Our blockade was not a close one, although it probably qualified as continuous. There were several reasons for this. The blockade line was intentionally located so as to be outside the range of Cuba's shore-based MIG fighters and IL-28 light bombers. At 500 miles, it was also out far enough to give us an operational cushion—time to decide whether any particular ship attempting to pass was actually to be stopped and boarded.

Some twenty-five Soviet-bloc vessels were headed toward Cuba at the time. A dozen turned back. In the end, the USSR withdrew its missiles. After twenty-seven days, the blockade was terminated. Twenty-five Soviet-bloc and twenty-three bloc-chartered merchantmen had been passed through the line, along with seven others.[1]

In law, blockade must be formally declared by a generally recognized international entity. To be wholly legal, it must also be effective, that is, close and continuous, not merely distant and/or occasional. It is the surest way of bringing about a decisive battle at sea, if one is to be fought at all. At this level, it is to be hoped not.

Not every blockade is by these standards legal. Nor is its ending necessarily a happy one. In the summer of 1989, Lebanon was a country divided into two camps—one Christian, one Moslem—each sworn to destroy the other as a political force. The outnumbered Christians stood alone. The Moslems were supported—even commanded—by troops and ships from Syria. Even fellow Arab governments called the mounting chaos genocide.

In August 1989, Christian Lebanon, with its ports of East Beirut and Juniyeh, was under blockade by Syria and its Moslem Lebanese allies. The illegally declared and only partially effective blockade had been imposed in March, in response to the Christian attempt to close the illegal Moslem ports of entry, mostly former yacht marinas, through which they were obtaining arms. This is more typical.

Every night a passenger ferry ran between the Christian enclave and Cyprus. Cargo ships brought in both civilian and military supplies without which the enclave—its back to the sea—would collapse, blockade or no.

On the twenty-ninth, Maltese flag *Sun Shield*, a small tanker carrying 700,000 gallons of gasoline, was six miles off the Lebanese coast, shuttling the fuel into Christian-held East Beirut from a supertanker offshore. *Sun Shield* was hit and set afire by radar-directed, shore-based Syrian artillery, and at least seven crew members were killed.

Sun Shield had successfully completed some seventy such runs in the past. This time it had been intercepted by a Syrian missile boat the day before, and warned to stop. It was the third such ship to be similarly hit by Syrian gunners. The international community remained impassive. Nothing was done.

CONVOY

Convoying merchant shipping—along a coast in the face of submarines, FACs, and aircraft; through a blockade; across waters in the face of raiders—is one of the standard wartime tasks, not least for these small navies. Convoys are collections of merchant ships sailed together for their mutual protection. Convoys are usually escorted, at least for critical runs.

Merchant shipping, almost guaranteed to be scarce, is one of the critical limiting factors governing all naval operations. Shipping not only provides bottoms for needed imports and exports, but also binds together the main sources of logistic support and the armed forces serving in distant overwater combat areas.

In WWI, the fundamental basis for the effectiveness of convoys was that they collected transitting shipping into just a few large groups, emptying most of the ocean of profitable targets. The unorganized individual U-boats seldom found them. Independent sailing was death, still.

In WWII, wolf pack tactics solved most of the U-boats' convoy location task, but a whole new generation of ASW and AA weapons, sensors, and tactics eventually made attacking escorted convoys just too costly.

There is not really either time or space here to discuss in detail whether or not it is wise to continue to convoy better submarines, and missiles, in the face of satellite-based sea surveillance systems. There is a school that hold all of the usual objections (delay of shipping, strain on port facilities, too passive tactics, etc.). It adds that gathering targets into large groups, considering the tremendously increased firepower and guidance available to a hostile force today, just makes the problem of the attacker that much simpler. The chances of any convoy are zero.

On the other hand, if close naval escort is to be given, if mines are to be swept ahead, then convoys are a must. Convoys not only concentrate the targets, they concentrate the defense. They make maximum use of those few, always scarce resources that are liable to be at hand.

The most tragic shipping disaster of WWII—the near-annihilation by U-boats and planes of convoy PQ17—was caused by the scattering of a convoy. In 1942, on the eve of the battle for Stalingrad, a convoy of thirty-five ships left Iceland for the long voyage around Norway's North Cape to Murmansk. The convoy was escorted at first by a powerful fleet, including battleships and carriers, but these were withdrawn midway. In London, Churchill brooded endlessly over the convoy's safe arrival. In Moscow, Stalin waited impatiently for the arms it carried.

Three weeks later, eleven battered and lonely ships limped into Russian ports. Two drifted in later. Of these thirteen ships, only two were genuine independents; the other eleven formed themselves voluntarily into small groups which were escorted by those corvettes and trawlers left behind when the larger escorts abandoned them. Two ships only from these rump miniconvoys were sunk. But nineteen ships that proceeded alone when the convoy was scattered went to the bottom, picked off at the enemy's leisure.[2]

During the three years between 1940 and 1943, in the Mediterranean, convoys also proved themselves. Italian convoys running to North Africa were evidently limited by geography to a quadrilateral bounded on the north by a line between Cape Bon and the Strait of Otranto, and on the south by the coast from Tripoli to Tobruk. Supply routes to Libya could only originate from Italy proper or from Sicily, and could only terminate at Tripoli, Bengazi, or Tobruk (as long as they were held). Often only Tripoli was left in Axis hands, forming in that event the tip of a funnel down which all shipping went. This everyone knew. Hunting was easy.

During 1987–88 in the Persian Gulf, merchant convoys were similarly limited. All shipping had to enter and exit the gulf through the Strait of Hormuz. Khor Fakkan—a United Arab Emirates port just outside the strait—was the usual holding point for inbound ships "under orders," and the makeup point for convoys. Inside, the western (Arab) waters were too shallow for deep draft traffic, the eastern (deep) ones were in the Irani prohibited area. Kuwait-bound convoys were therefore effectively restricted to a single de facto fairway along the gulf's main axis no wider than a large river. This everyone knew, too. Mining was a relatively simple matter.

Convoys in these waters tend to be small—two to eight ships. This is mandated by four factors: the constricted sea room, the operational requirements, a general shortage of ships, and the generally limited unloading/loading capacities of small arrival ports at one end or the other. Convoys tend to be direct, making a dash straight from one port to the other and back. They tend, too, to be frequent—not regular—spaced at the unloading pace of the recipient port.

In these waters, convoys normally sail in line ahead. This is hardly a matter of choice. Convoys sail as close inshore as they can. Cleared channels will be narrow. Ships must be led in and out by minesweepers, and each ship must follow in the wake of the one ahead. Column it is.

Escort numbers vary with the threat, and with the importance of the cargoes. Nonetheless, independently sailing ships are always at risk. At the very least, mission-essential units must be adequately escorted, whatever adequate means.

In extreme emergencies, critical ammunition, fuel, food, and personnel may have to be moved on naval combatants, faster and better able to defend themselves. Their cargo capacities are relatively small, however, and their ability to maneuver or fight with cargo on board is much less.

In the event, the decision to convoy or not will probably at this stage have to be made on the basis of a careful balancing of many diverse factors. Some of the relevant questions might be:

1. Are there any escorts in fact available? How near are they? What are their capabilities? What will the rules of engagement have to be?

2. Could peacetime escort of shipping be considered provocative by one side or the other?

3. Would employing an international escort help take the political sting away from an outside naval presence?

4. Would an international neutrality patrol effectively help deter trouble?

5. How able, relatively, are the merchant ships to take care of themselves?

6. What alternatives are there, to ensure safe and timely arrival?

Air cover is not always available, often because of organizational difficulties and concomitant absence of liaison. If it is present, cover will be scant and perhaps only for a portion of the run. Frequent changes of course, laying smoke (even at night), and an active AA defense at least minimize losses.

Operational factors are thus also a factor in keeping the size of most convoys down. Maneuvering a convoy at speed at night, in smoke, or both in constricted sea room is generally possible only if the formations are simple and easy to handle. For this, nothing beats a short, single column of homogeneous ships.[3]

THE SEA AND THE LAND

Historically, the close interaction between operations ashore and afloat has been no more evident than in the best known narrow sea, the Mediterranean. There the littoral powers have always as a matter of course devised war plans integrating sea and land operations, each dependent on and supporting the other. Successes and failures in one area react immediately on the other.

This had been a strategy validated by results. The fleets had convoyed and landed the armies. The armies had seized bases to be utilized by the fleets to support the next advance. The modern addition of air power only strengthened the basis of the practice, the radius of action of the planes involved setting the limits to the permissible distance between bases. Even in World War II, after a two-year seesaw campaign on land and sea, it was not until the Allies cleared North Africa that they gained command of the inland sea.

During the course of any future war in these waters, the same rules will apply. The capture of forward bases and the launching therefrom of further amphibious landings to seize new bases will continue to be a *sine qua non* of success. Forward-looking navies will be organized, trained, and equipped with this in mind.

Since on the narrow seas events on land have such an important, direct, and continuing effect on what happens at sea, and vice versa, staffs have to follow the military situation with a wider than normal eye to the whole picture. Unexpected opportunities are created and seized or lost, by the fleet at sea or the army shore. Both must be sensitive to the other's interest in this.

Such is not always the case. In World War II, during Operation Barbarossa (1941), Moscow was a main German objective. Moscow lay 670 miles east from the nearest land frontier, in Poland. The *Wehrmacht* took this route. Yet from Leningrad, behind the border defenses at the bottom of the Gulf of Finland, Moscow is only 400 miles away. Its capture would have turned the Moscow defense. It would have isolated Archangel and Murmansk, to the north. The Germans commanded the Baltic but failed to exploit this enormous strategic fact.

Power projection is the extension of the influence of seapower from the sea to the land, by means of amphibious landings, naval bombardment by gun or missile of coastal installations, and/or bombing by carrier planes. Prior sea control is always a must. Projection today is likely to be highly selective in nature, simply because it is limited by the number of available and liftable troops, supplies, and munitions. The most likely targets are thus military, or at least operational ones.

In narrow sea wars, any force launched from the sea for a limited objective ashore will be executing some variation of the amphibious strike. Such strikes can be employed to force an enemy to disperse his forces, divert his attention, or deny him use of vital equipment or facilities. They can remind an opponent that the war is still on. They can encourage allies.

Amphibious forces can temporarily secure a littoral state's capital or other seat of political or economic power, in addition to striking purely military targets. Where political power rests in the hands of only a small ruling elite, political targets have greater value than military ones. Such forces can rescue nationals trapped in hostile hands. They can prepare the way for follow-on forces.

Naval organizations are well suited for the *coup de main*. Most of the world's urban centers are located within ten miles of a coastline. Governments, embassies, commercial airfields and port facilities, as well as most other U.S. interests are usually found in or near these centers.

Power projection, however, can be much more subtle or even low key than this. Projection can be sea-based counterinsurgency. Overland movement in most Third World countries is inhibited by restrictive terrain and poor roads. In such an environment, a mobile sea-based force can readily outmaneuver insurgent (or counterinsurgent) units operating in the coastal plains or river deltas. Since few irregular movements possess a credible antiship capability, an amphibious force is able to operate at sea with relative impunity.

Britain's confrontation with Indonesia on Borneo and the surrounding area over formation of Malaysia began in 1962. It all started as police action to put down a local brigand and at its height was almost a war. Both sides had their own reasons for pretending this was not war. Neither wished to develop full-scale hostilities, at any point.

Involved among others in what turned out to be a joint affair were the Royal Marine Commando Brigade; its associated commando carriers, helicopters, and landing craft to provide troop mobility; and minesweepers for patrol, closing the north coast against waterborne infiltrators and arms.

Borneo's rivers were often the key to penetration of the island's interior. Early on, local ramp lighters became ad hoc assault craft, the minesweepers doing the converting and providing crews. Naval landing craft soon joined in.

Singapore provided a large, conveniently placed base with a relatively safe and easy line of communications to north Borneo. It furnished logistic support, shipbuilding and repair yards, rest and recreation for all units during the entire trouble. It housed communications and headquarters.

Shipping through the important straits and waters surrounding Indonesia was not ever interfered with. Innocent passage was respected. There were nonetheless tense periods when Britain, to assert this right, purposely sailed its men o'war through them.

In 1964, the Indonesians launched an attack from Sumatra across the Straits of Malacca, striking for a foothold on the Malayan mainland. A flotilla of small craft managed to land some one hundred guerrillas, the first of several such attempts. All failed.

It took a sizable joint military operation—primarily ashore—to put this all down, but down it was by 1966, four years later. Sea-based counterinsurgency played a large part. This too was a projection of power, a quietly successful one.[4]

MAHAN REDEFINED

Despite the U.S. Navy's belief that Neptune is God, sea-power the only true church, and Mahan the prophet, the admiral overstated his case. Command of the sea has never been an absolute, being much too broad a concept to be operationally really useful. As Corbett pointed out, in most situations neither side has command. Modern naval (post-Mahanian) thinkers have, therefore, developed redefinitions of the term, considered better to reflect the real world.

Sea control is one of these redefinitions. Less than command of the sea, it is the ability successfully to execute a given operation (destroy an enemy task group, blockade its ports, pass a convoy through, project force) to, from, and in a given body of water for at least a limited period of time. It is the ability to prevent significant interference by an enemy during that time. Theoretically, this could develop into command, if control extended long and far enough.

Sea denial, on the other hand, is the ability to prevent such use by an enemy. It is the mirror image of sea control. Sea denial does not provide for exploitation of the sea by the denying power, only that its enemy not exploit it. It is the resort of the second best. Even so, it too only applies to certain parts of the sea for a certain time. Surface units may be denied such use, but not submarines or planes.

Sea control is three-dimensional, beginning on the surface and reaching into the sky above and the depths down under. Sea denial may be sufficient for a land power when opposed by seapower. Sea control is always essential to a seapower, some place, sooner or later.

Thus, in World War II, the Allies in Europe, although clearly possessing naval superiority, were never able totally to blockade the Mediterranean, the west coast of the European continent, or the Baltic using surface-oriented seapower alone. All of these are narrow seas, of course. Air power and ASW had to be thrown in for them to exercise any control at all.

In these waters, adding large surface ships to a force may not increase its capability or buy security. Without air cover, adequate AA defenses, and ASW, it may only increase its vulnerability by unnecessarily adding to the number of potential high-value targets presented to the enemy. Witness U.S. losses during only a relatively short involvement against a weak enemy in the Persian Gulf (1987–88). Shallow water and the inevitable political constraints just make things worse.

Yet, as was very clearly demonstrated in the Falklands (1982), where a sufficient V/STOL and missile-equipped surface fleet is able and willing to take the almost certain heavy losses, it can operate successfully within a hostile air environment. Air supremacy is a relative and inexact thing.

In successful limited war, geographic conditions must allow the attacker to restrict the amount of force with which he has to deal. Islands, peninsulas, and jungle or desert-backed coastal strips perfectly meet these conditions; they are easily isolated by a strong navy, leaving only the defending garrison already in place to be faced. In sub-limited war, such preconditions are normally reinforced by the paucity of the forces brought to bear on scene by either party.

In these waters, as a rule, operational success builds on variations of one basic scenario. A specially tailored task group sweeps suddenly in from over the horizon, asserts control within a predetermined area for a carefully calculated minimum period of time, and there does whatever it was sent to do. Its control will ordinarily only be the result of locally superior force, brought in by surprise. It may not extend beyond the planned minimum time. It may not be expected to.

For example, in 1941, French Indochina Naval Forces consisted of one obsolescent light (6-inch gun) cruiser, eight old flying boats, four assorted colonial gunboats, plus several hydrographic vessels, and river gunboats. Light cruiser *Lamotte-Picquet* and the four gunboats were formed into a coastal force of sorts (in column they must have looked a little like Snow White and the Seven Dwarfs).

An undeclared border war with Thailand—Japan's puppet, joining those eager to capitalize on occupied France's weakness—had begun. Thailand laid claim to areas of Cambodia along the right bank of the Mekong, and Bangkok planned to dictate revisions of that border.

Thailand had become a not inconsiderable military power, on paper at least. It boasted 150 combat-capable aircraft. Its navy counted two modern armored coast defense (8-inch gun) ships, two gunboats, about ten modern torpedo boats, and lesser craft, far outclassing the French. Its navy was, however, totally untried.

The motley French "fleet" was ordered to take Thai pressure off very hard-pressed French troops. In mid-January, a naval flying boat successfully located a hostile force (the two coast defense ships and three of the torpedo boats). The Thais were gathered in an anchorage in the Koh-Chang Islands, off the southwest coast, into which there were several entrances (and exits). From there they were covering the right flank of the invading troops. There they were vulnerable. The French sailed.

On the seventeenth, the French struck. Making their final run-in during the night, they split into three task units—the light cruiser by itself, the two larger gunboats, and the two small old gunboats—so as to cover each exit, and at dawn burst in. In the course of a 105-minute hide-and-seek played in the grey mists and half light, they successfully sank all three Thai destroyers and seriously damaged both coast defense ships, without loss to themselves. The French were then forced to withdraw in face of the Thai air threat.

Japan at this point thought it prudent to step in and "mediate" in favor of the Thais. Without doubt, the ad hoc French force had bought Hanoi better terms than it might otherwise have gotten. This was sea control at its temporary and local best. Koh-Chang proved to be the force's swan song. The cruiser had soon to be laid up.[5]

GUADALCANAL

A year and-a-half later, at Guadalcanal (1942–43), the United States saw a perhaps more familiar example of longer term sea control. In mid-1942, the navy's South Pacific force was ordered to prepare to seize Guadalcanal (and Tulagi), to halt the booming Japanese drive on New Caledonia, Fiji, and Queensland. This time initial local sea control was to be turned into permanent control.

The Japanese were everywhere still on the strategic offensive. They exercised full control of the South Seas and were beginning to work on an airfield on Guadalcanal. In May they had seized nearby Tulagi, using it as a seaplane base. Only the communications line to Australia was still ours, and that was under threat.

U.S. preparations were hasty and forces available few. There was a three-carrier supporting force. There was an amphibious force of 16,000 marines embarked in transports, covered by six heavy cruisers, one light cruiser, and nineteen destroyers.

Everything went well, for a time. Surprise—essential to a successful assault against a hostile shore—was complete. The landings on August 7 were effected in full daylight against slight opposition, and the incomplete airstrip taken. We were too few to occupy the whole island.

The Japanese at Rabaul responded at once. They hurriedly assembled a scratch task group—five heavy cruisers, two light cruisers, and one destroyer—to run us off. They began air strikes, bombers with fighter cover. Their navy's plan was to close our beachhead in the small hours of the ninth, attack the covering warships, shoot up the transport area, and retire.

The evening before, we had withdrawn our carrier force well to the south, depriving our landing force of air cover. The still only partly unloaded transports had no choice but to follow. Only the covering force was left. In a thirty-two–minute battle, the enemy sank four of our cruisers, at almost no cost. Then they pulled back.

The first flights of marine aircraft arrived at Guadalcanal strip on the fifteenth. On the same day, the marines received their first reinforcements—aviation gas, ammunition, and ground crew—via three destroyer transports. These returned on the twentieth with rations.

During the twelve days following the Japanese victory at Savo Island, the Japanese could easily have run us off. They were strong enough to have asserted full sea (and air) control. They failed to exploit their opening. They brought in their forces piecemeal. By night they bombarded our shore positions, including the strip. They fought inconclusive battles at sea. It soon worked out that we exercised control of local waters during daylight—thanks to our superiority in the air—and the Japanese exercised it at night. Guadalcanal became a battle of attrition.

In the end, our navy extended its control of Solomons' waters to twenty-four hours a day, as we built up our strength there. We finally cleared the whole island. Our tenuous foothold in the Solomons became secure. What might have turned into only a spoiling attack resulted in a base supporting further advances.[6]

As can be seen, a stronger navy can generally impose its own pace on a battle. A weaker one, too weak for the tasks at hand and to the enemy, will take losses relatively greater than those incurred by the enemy. Reinforcements then arrive as replacements. This the Japanese did not learn until too late.

MISSIONS AND TASKS

The roles of all navies (including here coast guards) may be expressed in the form of missions (basic statements of a navy's reason for existence) and tasks (that which must be done to accomplish the assigned mission). Large navies may be divided, and become several small ones. When this is the case, they have more than one mission. Small navies usually really have only one military-oriented core mission, expressed in terms such as, "to command the sea approaches to the territory." How this command is to be gained and exercised constitutes the supporting tasks. Navies also exist simply to enhance a country's prestige, remember.

The tasks of the average small navy can be easily identified. In most cases they are explicitly assigned in a formal statement of functions by their own government; in those cases where they are not explicit, they are implicit. They are, in any case, many.

In both peace and war, these small navies are primarily responsible for patrol of the coastline—including canals, rivers, and lakes—to prevent the smuggling of goods, drugs, and arms, and the illegal movement of persons; for fisheries protection; and for search and rescue. Some are to carry out civic action programs. All are to render assistance to other military services in the maintenance of internal security.

In time of war, these navies are to defend against attack from the sea. They are to destroy local enemy naval forces. They are to protect shipping and oil rigs. They are to support other military and police services. Many are also to conduct minor amphibious operations and/or are otherwise to harass the enemy.

These navies are to defend their coasts and escort coastal convoys. They are to raid. Beyond that, they are to do what they can to damage the enemy.

For some of the small navies, these tasks are modified—expanded or contracted or shifted—as a result of commitments to regional alliances or mutual defense agreements. Witness Belgium, NATO's designated minesweeping specialists. The basic tasks nonetheless remain; the requirement to operate as part of a larger force is simply added on.

It takes a great deal of time, history, people, money, and resources—and blood, sweat, and tears—to build up a real navy. Constructing ships is a slow business, taking as long as five to ten years, the training of seamen-fighters an even slower one. It may be an exaggeration to say that intentions can change overnight; it is not one to say that threats can change from latent to actual in a very short space of time. But from a cold start, few of these navies—especially in the Third World—can be considered as being capable. They are unable fully to operate many of their ships, unable fully to support any policy. Some are not even aware of their severe technical and operational limits. It may take a war to teach them. Wars are the great auditors of navies.

Drunk with the heady writings of Mahan and other Great Power navalists, we see our early theories of limited maritime operations based on defense of the coast and commerce raiding as having hindered the development of a proper U.S. naval policy. For us, eventually command of the sea had to be the aim. But what other early choice did we have? What other one does a small navy still have?

It is in the narrow seas that the small navies really come into their own. Here both the capabilities and the roles of the small navies are sharpened. Here the two critical elements—the seas and the navies—are synergistic, one reinforcing the importance of the other. The narrow seas are in effect all inshore waters, remember.

MAYAGUEZ

Now, the battle for the first salvo remains an important factor in any contingency plan. Although in any armed conflict at sea the political and legal premium in not actually firing the first shot is high, and circumspection is a feature of the early stages of any such conflict, the smaller states have not always been restrained by custom. The rules of international law being so easily interpreted to support widely different views, their restraint is nil.

There is an unfortunate but growing tendency today for lesser states which see themselves as threatened to seize and hold even neutral merchantmen hostage against an unknown future, or as actual leverage against others. This happens at Suez, for instance. It happened in the Shatt-al-Arab, in 1980, also. It will happen again.

In May 1975, SS *Mayaguez*, a U.S. flag merchantman en route to Hong Kong–Thailand, on innocent passage through then-Communist Cambodian waters, was seized by a Cambodian patrol boat. The ship and her crew were held for two days. U.S. reaction was swift and sharp. A small marine assault unit was landed on a nearby island, searching for the crew. Naval vessels were moved in, and air strikes hit both the island and mainland opposite. *Mayaguez* was recovered, the crew released unharmed. Further reprisal was not needed.[7]

U.S. casualties in this action were severe: sixty-five killed and wounded. Nonetheless, the United States had demonstrated that despite its withdrawal from Vietnam, it was still able and willing to protect its interests at sea. We had compelled release of the ship and crew. We had not become a paper tiger. No second performance was needed.

Surprise is in any case critical to success in battle here. October 1946, two British destroyers struck mines laid without warning by Albania in Corfu Channel. Corfu Channel had heretofore been considered an international strait. By mining these destroyers, Albania unilaterally closed it. The British were completely taken aback.

Crises are dynamic situations that present only fleeting opportunities to exercise influence, so one's forces must always be ready, close at hand. Crises demand locally superior forces, the ability to control the air, to sweep the sea, and to move ashore, at once. Anything less is bluff. Anything less leads to longer, more expensive hostilities.

When hostilities actually break out, the first combat units to be turned loose are the aircraft, the FACs, and the submarines. Reserves are called up. Mines are laid at once, offensively as well as defensively. Convoys are formed and escorted. Coordinated ASW operations—based on radar, sonar, convoy, and planes—are relied on to counter enemy submarine efforts. Both sides probe for the enemy's weak points.

But then most navies face this. It is just that here, with time and distance so compressed, these opening tasks take on a special urgency. Sufficient mobile forces to dictate the direction and tempo of operations must be at once concentrated, if they in fact exist.

Things seldom work out in such an orderly manner, however. Ordinarily, the battle rapidly turns into a melee, with everything possible going on at once. Operational decisions are made on the basis of always incomplete information, as both sides grope through Clausewitz' fog of war, each for the other.

Navies are to fight. For the lesser navies, to be effective against an almost always larger opponent, this involves immediately bringing to bear everything relevant from whatever service, including their own, and making the most of it. Commercial and private aircraft become reconnaissance and observation planes. Car ferries become minelayers, trawlers minesweepers. Mobile artillery and missiles close down enemy ports within reach. For this, prior planning is absolutely essential. These navies cannot afford to overlook even one asset, victory coming to the one managing to use anything and everything, military and commercial, at hand. This goes against a natural inclination to conserve every precious, effectively irreplaceable resource against another day.

A navy too weak to win and keep command of the sea by large-scale offensive operations but still possessing secure bases may yet be dangerous. It carefully avoids actions risking its decisive defeat but rather assumes an active offensive defense. This is the classic role of the fleet-in-being.

Such a navy can dispose its available combat assets along its coast, forming scattered small task groups. Always assuming adequate air cover, these units can break out at night or during other periods of low visibility, randomly, to strike isolated enemy forces, especially if that enemy's LOC parallels the coast for any significant distance. Conceivably, this could sooner or later bring about a more even overall balance of forces. In the meantime, the enemy will find maintaining its control an expensive effort.

In war, deterrence still applies. It works to prevent or at least slow down escalation of either the intensity of the war—the number of troops or the weapons used—or the geographic extent of the area taken in, or both. It works to place a cap on what further fighting is worth. It works against third parties, to keep them benevolently neutral or even just out of the fighting altogether. At sea, this is a navy task.

Maritime power then is the ability to use the sea, in peace and war, commercially as well as militarily. States go to war to gain—or maintain—this power. Components of this power are a coast guard, a navy, a merchant marine, and a fishing fleet. Insofar as they exist, that is. Navies are the cutting edge of this power. They do not, however, operate in a vacuum.

NOTES

1. Elie Abel, *The Missile Crisis* (Philadelphia: J. B. Lippincott, 1966), passim.

2. David Irving, *The Destruction of Convoy PQ17* (New York: Simon and Schuster, 1968), pp. 290–304.

3. Aldo Cocchia, *The Hunters and the Hunted* (Annapolis, MD: U.S. Naval Institute, 1958), pp. 93–115.

4. Michael Carver, *War Since 1945* (New York: G. P. Putnam's Sons, 1981), pp. 12–27.

5. (Admiral) Romé, *Les Oubliés du Bout du Monde* (Paris: Editions Maritimes & d'Outre-Mer, 1983), pp. 66–75.

6. Samuel Eliot Morison, *The Two-Ocean War* (Boston: Little, Brown, 1963), pp. 164–82.

7. Roy Rowan, *The Four Days of Mayaguez* (New York: W. W. Norton, 1975), passim.

4

The Cutting Edge

THE NEW WAR

In October 1967, the Levant was reasonably quiet, resting in one of its cease-fire modes. The Arabs kept testing the water, however. The Israelis kept a destroyer patroling back and forth some thirteen miles off Port Said, to keep an eye on things in the Mediterranean's far southeast. No active hostilities were under way.

One day, without warning, four Soviet-built naval surface-to-surface guided missiles were fired at the destroyer from two also Soviet-built Egyptian *Komar* class fast attack boats (FACs) which appeared just outside Port Said.

With only seconds to respond, patroling old British-built Israeli destroyer *Eilat* could do little to defend itself. Three of the Styx missiles hit their intended target, sinking it. There was nothing left for the fourth to hit.

Thus was announced the fiery arrival of a whole new era in naval weapons and tactics. Missiles fired from a small platform by operators seeing their target only as a blip on a radar screen had destroyed a ship ten times the size of their own craft. More was soon to come.

In mid-May 1970, wooden-hulled fishing boat *Orit* was working off El Arish (northern Sinai). The trawler's four-man crew was concentrating on their nets and did not notice the bright light lifting over the western horizon and speeding silently in their direction through the night sky. Two Styx missiles exploded nearby in quick succession, then two more. The two crewmen, still alive, abandoned their boat and swam ashore to tell their story.

The Egyptians had demonstrated that the Styx homed not only on a 2500-ton steel-hulled destroyer but also on a 70-ton wooden boat. For the moment there was nothing the Israelis could do about it except avoid providing the enemy with surface targets.

Only three years later, in the so-called Yom Kippur 1973 war, Israel showed the world that it could not only adopt but better the weapons of this new era. Well covered by the Israeli Air Force, the navy completely cleared the eastern Mediterranean of the Syrian and Egyptian fleets, thereby preventing large-scale attacks upon the country's vulnerable coast, and keeping its vital sea communications open. It did the same in the Red Sea.

By the time of the 1973 war, Israeli naval order of battle included thirteen SAAR class FACs—eleven missile-armed boats, two gun boats. These were "the boats of Cherbourg," and were to firmly establish the parimeters of this new era. Egypt on the other hand counted fourteen FACs—twelve OSAs, two KOMARs. Syria had three OSAs and six KOMARs. Overall this gave the Arabs a two-to-one margin of strength.

Arab Russian-built FACs carried Styx missiles, the OSAs four each, the KOMARs two. Israeli missile boats were armed with Israeli-built Gabriel missiles, some with six, some with eight. The Arab boats had no electronic warfare (EW) capability, the Israelis did.

Israel's FACs were based at Haifa, roughly equidistant (one hundred miles) from either Syria or Egypt. Israel thus enjoyed the advantage of interior lines. Concentrating first on the most dangerous enemy, Israel struck first at Syria, then Egypt. This kept the odds closer to even. Two battles were thus fought, one off Latakia (Syria), the other off Damietta (Egypt), one right after the other.

Israeli FACs were not only outnumbered but outranged by the Arab missiles. The 30-mile range Styx could hit the Gabriel-armed boats long before the latter's 13-mile missiles could reach them. The decisive factor, however, proved this time to be the Israeli monopoly of EW. It was that which enabled Israeli FACs successfully to elude a total of fifty-four Styx missiles while themselves sinking at least eight Arab boats, and perhaps two more, all without a single casualty of their own.

The Israeli Navy dominated Levant waters for the rest of the 1973 war, exercising as close a command of the Mediterranean Sea as anyone could expect. This, although only FACs had met FACs. The Israelis were the only ones prepared to exploit fully the new weaponry. Navies everywhere paid close attention.[1]

THE WIDER VIEW

In these waters, hostilities or no, ships and craft, naval and merchant, operate under all sorts of geographic, political, military, and commercial constraints. They are often tethered for long periods to known locations, sometimes in port, or move regularly down known channels in close proximity to prominent landmarks like promontories or headlands. They are readily located and attacked by an enemy who has a free choice of means.

To meet the full range of threats posed by such an enemy calls for a balanced fleet—balanced in narrow seas and small navy terms, of course. It must be configured to operate among the rocks and shoals, the characteristically shallow depths and tortuous channels found in the narrow seas. The core of such a balanced fleet will be formed by V/STOL carriers, destroyers, frigates, coastal submarines, FACs, mine warfare craft, and amphibious lift. Cruisers, corvettes, and the like will be added as they are required, available and as opportunity offers.

FACs are always a threat. They attack in numbers, maybe in conjunction with aircraft, trying to saturate the defense. Engines throttled down to avoid unnecessary noise and large wakes, they surprise with missile, torpedo, and gun—and dash away. Or they move in quietly, sowing their mines along the inshore channels and harbor approaches, and steal away.

In surface gun actions, the primary task is to place the largest possible weight of metal on the enemy in the shortest possible time. Sustained combat, however, is for FACs just not in the cards. There are strict limits on the amount of ammunition, and fuel, that can be carried on board. Fights blaze up suddenly and are almost as quickly over.

Torpedo and missile actions present the same picture. There may be two torpedoes, with two reloads. There may be four or six missiles. Once they are fired, there are no more. FACs shoot and scoot.

FACs use topography and weather to hide them from the enemy for as long as possible, allowing him to draw near. Further tactics call for the use of EW (electronic warfare—using flares and chaff) to jam or trick its radar and IR (infra-red), confusing the enemy concerning one's whereabouts. There may be a diversionary attack from a different direction, distracting attention. The FACs then pounce on the enemy somewhere within range from out of an electronic cloud, getting in the first salvo.

In the narrow seas, a gun- and missile-armed destroyer can perform the same leadership role for a squadron of FACs that a light cruiser does for a squadron of destroyers. The destroyer provides the overall command platform and heavy firepower; the FACs find and flush out the targets, and finish them off. The combination can be deadly.

While few, submarines when present cause an inordinate amount of furor. They themselves avoid coming close inshore, normally, feeling too exposed there. They prefer the deeper water for their work. They use mines to drive shipping out of the shallower areas, and wait offshore at traffic choke points, preferably at night, for ships to come to them. They then apply torpedo, gun, or today even perhaps missile. Inordinately large ASW efforts inevitably result.

CONVOY ESCORT

Convoy escort teams—surface escorts, submarines, aircraft— are still centered around the surface platform. It is after all the use of the surface of the sea that is the main prize. Only surface escorts possess the required long-term, all weather, 24-hour-a-day capability. It is on one of these that the officer in tactical command rides. Surface escorts now carry long-range AA, antiship, and ASW sensors and weapons powerful beyond their size. Recent technological advances have enormously increased the range and speed at which escort actions are fought.

For a surface ship—even an armed one—to be caught out alone in daylight in a battle area without air cover and ASW protection is tantamount to suicide. Ships either move in convoy, keep well out to sea, or stay close within defended areas— or move at night or under other conditions of low visibility. Convoy is the usual answer, where it is possible, as we have seen.

Defense against low-flying aircraft and aircraft-launched missiles is three-tiered, organized in depth. First, fighter planes, operating farthest out, would attempt to knock down the enemy plane before it had a chance to launch its missiles. Second, surface escorts would employ their own AA missiles against any plane that escaped or missiles that were launched, providing area (long-range) and point (short-range) defense. Third, ships would bring their own close-in weapons system (CIWS) into action against anything still coming in.

ASW defense is parallel. Again, a layered system must be regarded as ideal, because no single element will be able to provide total cover. For a merchant convoy under escort, a layered defense will provide security in depth, both close in and farther out.

Fixed-wing aircraft (land-based maritime patrol or ASW carrier-borne) operating many miles distant, drop sonobuoy barriers to develop a general picture of the submarines approaching the convoy. They attack them when they can, using depth charges and ASW torpedoes. Closer in, helos use dipping sonor and magnetic anomaly detector (MAD) to more closely locate those submarines. They then drop depth charges or light-weight torpedoes, either on their own or at the direction of surface ships, to sink those subs or at least discourage attack. Surface escorts with hull-mounted or towed array sonar—carrying depth charges and heavy torpedoes—are the last-ditch defense.

The "defended lane" concept seems for escorts to be the best operational answer to the missile-armed submarine. Under this concept, a mix of ASW forces paralleling a convoy keeps a moving passive sonar watch in waters on either side of a convoy's route. The sides of this defended lane are set at a greater distance (let's say, 250 miles) from the track of the convoy than the effective range of enemy sub-launched antiship missiles (200 miles).

A close escort using active sonar usually also surrounds the convoy, as still the best answer to the torpedo-armed submarine, although on occasion single or even small groups of fast merchantmen might attempt a dash without escort, on their own.

MINES

At the same time that it has worked to drive off surface fleets, technology has provided navies with substitute weapons with which to impose a blockade, de facto if not de jure. Aircraft-laid influence mines can quite effectively close off a coast or a specific port. Given, of course, that the target area is within range of the delivery aircraft, that the planes are able to lay the mines, and that enough mines to saturate the countermeasures are laid. If large numbers of mines are involved, shore-based air will have a role here, too.

Mine warfare is, however, almost never simply a plain, straightforward matter of laying offensive and defensive fields. It is here rather a matter of move and scheme, lie, plot, and countermove, with surprise always playing an important role.

In the Solomons in 1943, three U.S. destroyers quietly dropped a field of mines across Blackett Strait. Several days later three Japanese destroyers coming down the Slot as part of the "Tokyo Express" ran right into it. One was sunk. Two others were damaged, to be finished off next day from the air. Those approximately 240 mines—laid at night in tropical rain, without accurate charts—well demonstrated what a surprise field can do. The next time that was tried, the Japanese were ready with a flotilla of sweepers. They rushed out the next morning and cleared the mines without loss.

Paths have to be cleared through existing enemy (and even friendly) fields, and continually check-swept. Paths cleared by the enemy have to be closed again. Traps have to be set. They are.

Routine minesweeping is usually carried out using locally organized craft of opportunity—converted trawlers, tugs, offshore supply vessels, and the like. Problem areas beyond the capabilities of these craft are closed off to friendly traffic until they can be dealt with by the always too few professional experts, troubleshooting minesweeping and minehunting forces moving from area to area. In friendly waters, there is almost always the dark silhouette of one or more somewhere on the horizon.

Night surface actions are common among small forces, radar or no. In March 1945, Soviet planes attacked a small loaded German fuel tanker escorted by four motor minesweepers, on its way from Pillau to Libau in the Baltic. The planes sank the precious, irreplaceable tanker along with three of its escorts. German fighters then arrived and shot down eleven of the enemy, driving off the rest. Three German FACs out of Libau picked up the survivors, took them to base, then returned to the still-burning tanker.

It was by now night. The German FACs completely surprised nine Soviet boats looking for signalbooks or other material. In a fight lasting two hours, fought at 300 meters, the three German FACs sank two of the enemy, boarded another one, and took fourteen prisoners. The fuel was lost.

Night engagements are still common today. Light craft meet at sea, sometimes unexpectedly, engaged on separate tasks. One group might even actually be out hunting game, another escorting a convoy. There is a challenge, and a delayed or inadequate response. Radars go active. Throttles are shoved forward, right to the stops.

The night then all at once erupts with star-shells. Gunfire sends lazy ribbons of red or yellow-green tracer searching for the enemy. Missiles roar away in blinding explosions of light. The sea is furrowed by torpedoes on opposing tracks fired at close range. Radios open up, requesting information, transmitting urgent orders. Chaff blooms, ECM (electronic countermeasures) goes to work. Magnesium flares pop, decoys for heatseekers. The result can sometimes be devastating. But often in unexpected night actions, neither side may be seriously hurt. The craft eventually break off the action, probably out of ammunition, one by one.

Superior speed here as elsewhere enables units to concentrate against whatever target they think best, striking from whatever direction desired; to force battle; or to refuse it, at will.

The engagements thus die out as rapidly as they flare up. Both sides may continue on their way. The "winner"—if there is one—is the one whose tasks are the least interfered with.

BASES

Bases are the connecting link between fleet and shore. About bases, the three items of interest are their location, their defenses, and the facilities they offer. Bases can be identified as main and secondary, or as principal, operating, and advanced, according to use. In a short-legged world, bases like carriers are key to operations at any distance.

Even before hostilities begin, coast defenses are activated and selected ports defended. Main bases usually start with a protected anchorage of sufficient size. Any base must have that. Then come berthing, some sort of repair (yard) facilities, drydock, workshops, warehouses, barracks, and offices, and the ability to replenish the traditional bullets, beans, and black oil. An airfield, a hospital, and a communications station complete the complex along with such things as nearby oil storage tanks. To this the best bases add industrial support and a trained, willing work force—and facilities for crew rest.

None of this, however, is of much use unless the base is well located, central, or at (or near) straits and traffic choke points, or commercial ports. Well positioned, it allows a fleet to do more with less. Think of Germany's Kiel, in the Baltic, or France's Toulon, in the Mediterranean.

Advanced bases generally consist of an anchorage at which are stationed one or more auxiliary supporting ships. These last are perhaps only a single tender or barge, or maybe a tender and a small oiler, or even a small fleet train complete with a repair ship. These are in any event capable only of sustaining life, not embellishing it. Fuel, ammunition, food, water, basic stores, and only the most rudimentary running repairs are likely to be had. Unless co-located in a commercial or at least a fishing port, such bases thus offer little respite for tired men and belabored ships. They are often temporary in nature.

All bases must be secure. They may have to be defended, using troops, nets, mines, coast artillery, AA artillery, missiles, and planes. They must, therefore, be defensible with the forces at hand. The ability to secure a base has a direct bearing on how far forward it can be put. No base can be secure for longer than the time it takes for enemy air and naval power to gain control of the skies over and the seas around them.

Coastal surveillance and base defense are interdependent. Bases are likely to be advanced bases temporarily held. They are very exposed, even in less intense conditions. They need to be watched over.

MANPOWER

The first look at a navy's personnel must ordinarily be an overall one. Concerning personnel collectively, the items of interest are always three: numbers, training, and morale. Personnel ashore and afloat can be categorized as general service (deck and engineering), submarine, aviation, naval infantry (marines), shore engineering, administrative, medical, finance, and supply.

In the small navies, except for those of Western Europe and states like Israel, the enlisted men tend to be drawn from the semiliterate, technologically ignorant. Their training must begin with the most elementary items, and most never reach beyond a rudimentary grasp of what they need to know.

What are the officers like? Here one can be more individual. Is there an academy? How are officers schooled, beyond that?

In these organizations, the flag officer commanding and a small immediate group—his chief of staff, a deputy (operations), and a deputy (logistics)—often run the show on a day-to-day basis. There is little delegation of authority, and little flexibility. Modern ideas on management are little known. Efficiency and morale suffer.

In the Third World, there is often considerable graft, corruption, patronage, and nepotism, all of which strike at efficiency and morale, too. It is often by these means that political reliability—overridingly important—is secured, nonetheless.

What about the reserves? In the European navies and those of Westernized states like Israel, reserves play a critical role in any wartime mobilization. Are there any? If so, what are their numbers, training, and morale? How long would it take to activate them? How much additional time would it take to make them combat-ready?

In every navy, the officers and men who man the small inshore ships and craft tend to be a breed apart. Often they are reservists or hostilities-only types. In a different, earlier age, they would be buccaneers or privateers. They are worth their weight in gold.

They must instinctively know the value in battle of the weather gauge, even today. They must know the need to be up sun, down moon.

Emphasis here is placed upon personal leadership, first. Then come practical pilotage and d'ed reckoning, seamanship, and ship-handling skill. Gunnery, communications, and engineering are relatively direct. A taste for action does not hurt, either.

THE FALKLANDS

In April 1982, Argentina seized their Malvinas Islands, ousting the British after 150 years. Seventy-four days later, the British had the Falklands (Malvinas) back. This was the first high tech naval war in history. The Harrier V/STOL fighter-bomber and the Exocet guided missile were both used, as computer faced computer.

This, the largest sea-air conflict since WWII saw in the meantime the Argentine Navy land a marine assault battalion, support and cover the landing, and then bring in an army division to hold the gains.

The Royal Navy in response launched an amphibious counterassault from 8000 miles away, covering the whole operation with two V/STOL light carriers.

The Falklands are made up of about 200 islands lying loosely in the center of an arc with a radius of 400 miles, off Argentina's southeastern coast. For eight months of the year they are a country of mountainous seas and freezing fog; the rest of the time they are merely cool and wet. They are of considerable strategic, commercial, and emotional importance to both sides. Among other things, they are a key to a large slice of the Antarctic pie.

The Argentine seizure of the British Falkland Islands and their subsequent recovery by the Royal Navy (1982) provides us with a prime example of modern war between two lesser navies. Both countries and their navies qualified as regional powers, separated in this case by a third of the globe. This was, however, an atypical deep water narrow seas war, its essential characteristics being dictated by the requirement for larger ships with good sea-keeping qualities, and by the geography of the area.

In 1982, the Argentine Navy contained as its centerpiece a single aging light (small) 16,000-ton conventional flat-deck aircraft carrier, *25 de Mayo*. The remainder was mostly also second hand—a light cruiser, eight destroyers, three corvettes, a landing ship, auxiliaries, and service craft. It was balanced, well trained, and modernizing, if but slowly. It had several submarines, but they played little part in what took place.

The Royal Navy possessed two V/STOL carriers, two auxiliary V/STOL carriers, five destroyers, fourteen frigates, two amphibious warfare ships, submarines, and the usual assortment of auxiliaries available for deployment. It too was a well balanced force, superbly trained, with the arrogance of 400 years of victory behind it. It was backed by equal numbers of merchantmen taken up from trade.

For the Falklands operation, the Argentine Navy made up four task forces. The covering carrier force was positioned to the north of the islands. It was composed of *25 de Mayo* (flag), four destroyers, an oiler, and a tug. An amphibious force, including two destroyers, two of the corvettes, the landing ship, two transports loaded with a reinforced marine battalion, and a submarine, was to seize the islands. A third force was formed from a polar transport, a small detachment of marines, and the third corvette to take South Georgia, 800 miles southeast. The fourth task force—the cruiser and two destroyers—was positioned to the south of the Falklands.

The critical elements of the naval air arm were disposed as follows: on the carrier, an air group made up of ASW planes, eight A-4 attack planes, and some helos; ashore, the Super-Etendard squadron, armed with Exocet missiles, flying out of Commodoro Rivadavia; also ashore, several P-2 maritime patrol planes. The air force provided airborne refuelling when asked.

For the British, time was absolutely critical. Politically, the British government had to move before the first flush of internal popular support evaporated. Abroad, they had to act before world popular opinion could be mobilized against them. Winter, in an area where it is noted for its ferocity, was almost upon them. Its arrival would effectively delay any large-scale operations in the Falklands area until spring, leaving the Argentines in full control of their ill-gotten gains. Meanwhile, the international political machinery could be mobilized to stall any further use of force until Argentine occupation of the liberated islands was legitimized. For London, it was then or never.

The Argentine Navy successfully seized the islands, if against only slight opposition. The Navy then withdrew, preparing to meet the Royal Navy if the British reacted in kind and came to free the islands. Buenos Aires reorganized its fleet, forming it into three task groups. The carrier, a destroyer, and the three corvettes, plus an oiler made up the first. Five destroyers and an oiler formed the second. The cruiser, her two destroyers, and an oiler constituted the third.

But the Argentine Navy never met the British fleet full-scale, head on. The Argentine carrier apparently broke down, and its task group had to be withdrawn. When it was decided that the carrier was not likely to play any further significant role in the campaign, her three corvettes and oiler were detached, forming a fourth task group. A British submarine torpedoed the cruiser, and sank it. The destroyers joined the second task group as numbers four and five. But the Argentine fleet's heart had been taken out of it.

From then on, Argentine naval input to the war was to be limited to that provided by the naval air arm. The carrier's air group joined the Etendards ashore at Commodoro Rivadavia. Trained for *naval* air operations, it was these planes—in spite of near-insane flying by all pilots—that did most of the subsequent damage to British forces at sea.

The Royal Navy did come south, avenging angels taking only a month to build up their forces off the Falklands. South Georgia was liberated on the way. Then the Falklands were retaken. For the latter effort, a commando brigade was loaded and transported south, and then assault-landed in the islands. An army infantry brigade followed.

In just 74 days the Falklands campaign was all over. The day after the Argentine surrender and the islands came again under the crown, the first snow fell. The Royal Navy had successfully gained local control of the sea (largely by default), and then projected power down the North and South Atlantic from 8000 miles away.[2]

In the area of technical innovation, aircraft and their missiles led the way on both sides. Planes carried heat-seeking and radar-homing missiles for use against ground targets, ships, or other planes. In defense they could fire magnesium flares to confuse heat-seeking missiles, and they could jam radar. Some missiles had proxility as well as impact fuses, turning near misses into hits.

Of all the naval weapon systems employed by the British, the short-legged, sub- (or trans-) sonic V/STOL Harrier must be judged the best. It did not win them the war, but without it, the British would certainly have lost the war.

The Sea Harrier was classified as a single wing attack craft, with a wingspan of 25 feet, a length of 46 feet, and a height of 11 feet, weighing 23,100 lbs., capable of flying out at mach 0.96 (mach 1.2 diving). It had a practical maximum ceiling of 50,000 feet.

Taking off vertically, the Harrier's range with a full load of ordnance and fuel was fifty to one hundred miles; with a short takeoff run, it was 250 miles. There was a severe range/load tradeoff, but the Harrier can carry as much as 5000 lbs. of ordnance.

An eventual total of twenty-eight Sea Harriers and 14 RAF versions were deployed to the battle area. They flew CAP effectively, with air-to-air missiles and two 30-mm cannon. They flew reconnaissance and attack missions. They saved the day.

During this battle for the Falklands, a chastening grand total of eleven out of the twenty-seven British surface warships involved were either sunk or damaged by Argentine bombs or guided missiles. There were several reasons for this, all typical of war in the narrow seas.

British escorts were hindered in their freedom to maneuver by having to cover the landing and continue support of their amphibious element. They were also constricted by the 200-mile radius "exclusion zone" within and around which the fleet operated at sea, and by the narrowness of the key Falkland Sound itself. Basically, they were tied to the islands, relatively easy-to-find targets. They also lacked airborne AEW.

Despite all this, in this case the two British V/STOL light carriers operating together managed between them to perform most of the duties of a conventional flat top, even to limited force projection. In so doing, however, they continually exposed themselves to potential attack by Argentine carrier-borne and shore-based aircraft, land-based missiles, and submarines.

In the event, only shore-based aircraft and missiles materialized, although they succeeded in doing serious damage. Had the Argentine Navy been able to employ in addition either an effective carrier (it had one) or submarine (it had two)—or both—the British would have lost.

SEA-BASED/SEA-RELATED AIR POWER

In 1940, the British hurriedly assembled an expeditionary force and sent it off to Norway with the full might of the Royal Navy in support. The Germans had seized Norway. But by the time the fleet was deployed, the *Luftwaffe* was flying from captured Norwegian air bases in strength. Lacking adequate air support, the British were badly mauled. After two months they pulled out. The toll was too high; the fleet was being eaten up.

Before the Norwegian campaign was over, although few major warships were actually sunk by bombs alone, the Germans succeeded in sinking an aircraft carrier, two cruisers, one sloop, and nine destroyers. They damaged another six cruisers, two sloops, and eight destroyers, the majority through air attack.

The Norwegian campaign, followed by the attack on Taranto, the air seige of Malta, the Greek campaign, the operations off Crete—and then the attack on Pearl Harbor and the destruction of Force Z showed in and rammed home a new order of seapower. No surface fleet could any longer operate within range of an enemy—especially in the narrow seas—without at least temporary and local air superiority. No guns alone could any longer defend a fleet. No fleet could operate without either adequate organic aircraft or shore-based air cover.[3]

These points are still valid. In these waters, air power—sea-based or sea-related—comes into its own. Everything is within range, all the time. To survive, a battle group must include from somewhere an air increment adequate for defense, that is, CAP and ASW, under at least its own operational control. In these waters, to project power ashore a battle group must include from somewhere an air increment adequate not only for defense but also large-scale strike. Some or all of this air is often apt to be land-based, particularly with small navies.

Shore-based air—for reconnaissance, CAP, strike, or ASW—is too often overlooked. It can be effective. In WWII for instance, the German attempt to counter the British Atlantic blockade with one of their own based ultimately on the unrestricted use of submarines was eventually broken by land-based ASW-configured maritime patrol planes more than by any other single means. Land-based aircraft made far and away the most submarine kills, perhaps more than those by surface ships, submarines, and carrier planes combined. Navies tend to forget that.

In March 1943, a strong Japanese convoy departed Rabaul, in the Solomons, bound for Lae, New Guinea. Aboard were 7000 reinforcing troops in eight transports, escorted by as many destroyers. Lae was one of MacArthur's next objectives, and the convoy had to be stopped. It was.

Coming in from over Papua, U.S. and Australian Air Force land-based bombers caught the convoy in daylight, underway in the Bismarck Sea. Air force fighters drove off the Japanese CAP; others took out the airfield at Lae. Skip bombing at masthead height, the planes then sank seven out of eight transports and four of the escorting destroyers. Surface forces finished off the remaining transport the next day.

The Battle of the Bismarck Sea was one of the most devastating air attacks on ships of the entire war. The Japanese lost 3000 to 4000 troops. They never again risked a transport larger than a barge in waters dominated by U.S. air power.[4]

With light (possibly V/STOL) carriers, a small navy's local control of the sea is unquestionably enhanced, complicating attempts at extra-regional intervention and helping to intimidate smaller nearby states. Nonetheless, power projection based only on one of these light V/STOL carriers is not to be thought of except against the very weakest, most disorganized adversaries. With a single such carrier: AEW, yes. CAP, yes. ASW, yes. One-time necessarily small strike, especially with the advantage of surprise, yes. Sustained projection against an alert enemy of almost any strength, ordinarily no. Any on-board air group is going to be just too small for such work.

Two carriers working together are four times better than just one. Two carriers allow an operational division of labor, one of them concentrating on fighter management (CAP and AEW, perhaps even limited power projection, now), the other on ASW. Much more efficient operations thereby become possible.[5]

Air superiority provides at least local control of the air, allowing a force to do other things on the surface and from the surface. Today, it is a must.

In a set piece sea-air battle, aircraft carrier versus carrier or convoy, doctrine emphasizes that the primary concern of a fleet commander must be to establish and maintain air superiority over his own task group, and then over that of the enemy. This is usually accomplished with fighter combat air patrols (CAPs) flying cover over his task group, and with offensive sorties against enemy carriers and supporting airfields. He depends for effectiveness in this on adequate surveillance of the battle area.

To gain air superiority against a shore-based enemy, carrier-launched fighter sweeps strike his airfields, going for planes on the ground and in the air, for ground control, and for AA defenses, paving the way for bombers. Bombers then blast the fields, cratering runways, destroying support facilities, setting ammunition and fuel dumps on fire, paralyzing the fields. Standing fighter patrols continue to orbit and strafe, keeping the fields pounded down, "bouncing" anything that tries to use them.

In a set piece sea-air-land battle, say an amphibious landing, the offensive tasks of either carrier-borne or shore-based air units—or of them both, together—are three fold: first, to gain and keep that air supremacy over the battle area; then to isolate the target by cutting the sea approaches and air feeder routes into it; and last, to join the surface fight. These things are best carried out in the order given.

The United States was (re)taught the bitter truth of this during our landing at Lingayan (Luzon) in January 1945. The best method of suppressing enemy shore-based air in such an amphibious operation is on the ground, neutralizing its bases beforehand so that serious strikes cannot be mounted from them against us. Otherwise, as in the gulf, they will wait until we are fully committed before they hit us, catching us tied to the beaches, when the enemy cannot easily be dealt with and its targets are many. At Lingayan, Japanese fields were not taken out.

The defensive tasks of sea-based/sea-related air units are themselves to maintain control over their own task groups at sea and over bases ashore, including such additional naval forces as might be engaged in secondary holding tasks. Fighters regularly also escort offensive strikes. In so doing, they weaken the enemy's offensive strike capability, eventually wearing down its air threat.

As they execute these several tasks, air units need to keep full pace with events, alert to preventing the enemy from somehow (re)gaining the upper hand. Few battles are really set piece. Maritime patrol and ASW goes on the whole while.

Hostile sea-based/sea-related planes are in any case a continuous threat to any force in these waters, within range. Given time, a land-based enemy can always concentrate its available and perhaps overwhelming air (and missile) strength against any fixed target (a base or port) or one which imprudently remains immobile for too long (ships). A cooperating carrier establishes a threat from a different direction. Even a single opposing carrier makes its attack task a great deal more involved, offering the threat of much greater losses. They have to be one of the first things to be taken out by either side.

In 1944 in the Baltic, as the German *Kriegsmarine* was engaged in its desperate fighting withdrawal back into the homeland proper, we see a good example of this ability of land-based air to concentrate against fixed maritime targets. As could be expected—considering the exploding role of air power everywhere, as well as the Red Air Force's highly developed, hard-earned expertise in its tactical employment against land forces—the first and biggest single Soviet success against the Germans came ashore, in mid-December.

As the year came to a freezing end, *Luftwaffe* air support had become more and more scarce. Losses were not being replaced. Fuel was harder and harder to come by. Red aircraft then carried out a two-day mass attack on Libau, the largest port in the Kurland beachhead. The pocket was stuffed with refugees, troops, and logistic units, and the port with merchant and naval vessels. The Red Air Force managed, however, to sink only a total of four merchantmen, damaging eight others. Nonetheless, this attack cost them an even one hundred planes. Once the air defenses of the port were reorganized and strengthened, further air attacks there achieved nothing at all.

In the last four months of World War II (January to May 1945), the whole Allied campaign against German shipping in the Baltic reached an operational crescendo. The British RAF, the U.S. Air Force, Royal Navy carrier-borne aircraft, and light surface forces all becoming surplus to other tasks, target-hungry, went hunting for evacuation ships and their naval escorts. Mines were dropped in sufficient quantity, at long last. Everyone participated, finally overwhelming German defenses. Every joint and combined force ultimately was joined in, inflicting crippling losses in the west. The Soviet Navy and Air Force kept up the pressure in the east.

Loss patterns in this period followed expectations. Bombs and rockets accounted for the greater part of those merchant types lost (at least eighty-eight ships), with mines next (half as many), and torpedoes a distant third (ten). Losses were heaviest among those ships that were steaming inadequately escorted, or not escorted at all. Or were caught in port.

Every deliberate air strike properly requires three phases: prestrike reconnaissance; the strike itself; and poststrike reconnaissance to assess damage, if any. This can soak up a large number of aircraft, and the ideal is seldom attained by these small forces.

Small craft with limited AA armament and ammunition capacity, fishermen, and merchantmen of any size, make the softest targets. But if the enemy is willing to pay the price, any ship or craft within operational range is possible game.

Direct air attack by day is effective. Direct air attack at night is not, even with guided "smart" missiles, especially near shore or island-infested waters, or where there is a lot of neutral traffic.

Aircraft often attack in mass by day, but tend to hunt alone at night. Bomb and gun are still popular, but air-to-surface missiles are becoming increasingly available. Cheaply, too.

Land-based naval aviation and V/STOL carriers can provide often synergistic as well as sometimes competitive solutions to the problem of air support at sea. Shore-based maritime reconnaissance, for instance, can cover wider areas of the sea more quickly than sometimes even a carrier can. Airborne warning and command can then be brought into play, managing the joint battle.

Once a target is located, the carrier can bring its superior strike capability to bear. It can then easily move on to the next target, or loiter over the distant horizon until a new one is given.

CAVEAT EMPTOR

Interservice rivalries—even honest differences in strategic outlook—create serious fundamental obstacles to navy–air force cooperation in any form. Even in the sophisticated West they continue. Why in WWII were the German submarine pens in France and Norway not bombed during construction, when they were vulnerable, rather than later when they were not? Why was the mid-Atlantic convoy air cover gap allowed to continue long after the heavy long-range bombers to close it were flying? Evidently, air force priorities were elsewhere.

Shore-based planes from other than a naval air arm, while sometimes surprisingly high-tech, are, however, not as a rule as effective over water as naval air. Unless they are specially equipped and trained, serious deficiencies in weaponry, over-water navigation, reconnaissance and patrol procedures, recognition, and attack (including ASW) are all too common. Witness the Falklands. Bravery is not enough.

Not every target located from the air is necessarily attacked. Not at all. Pilot inexperience, contrary orders, too rigid orders, low fuel, and high risk can all conspire to create exceptions. So can recognition and interest problems. Misunderstandings abound.

In WWII, it was only in 1939, after much political infighting that the *Kriegsmarine* and the *Luftwaffe* reached an agreement on their wartime roles and missions. Under it, anything that flew belonged to the Luftwaffe. The Kriegsmarine was to exercise operational control of overwater air reconnaissance, and of tactical air during contact between naval forces. The Luftwaffe retained control of all else, including strikes against shipping in harbor and at sea, on shipyards and bases, and aerial minelaying.

All of the agreed dedicated maritime air units were never organized. The best maritime aircraft were never developed.

Luftwaffe radio frequencies and codes did not mesh with those of the navy. Air-delivered mines were badly designed. The Luftwaffe preferred to use bombs against ships, the navy torpedoes.[6] Italy did no better, Britain for years only marginally so.

Traditionally, the air force fights its own war. It can hardly seem the same one. Air force contributions to the navy battle have usually been limited to large-scale bombing and mining. As the Soviets have known for years, this can no longer be enough. The interservice cooperation problem remains a serious one, especially in the Third World.

For surface ships and craft, eternal paranoia is nonetheless always the price of survival.

NOTES

1. Abraham Rabinovich, *The Boats of Cherbourg* (Annapolis, MD: Naval Institute Press, 1988), pp. 205–28.

2. Charles W. Koburger, Jr., *Sea Power in the Falklands* (New York: Praeger, 1983), pp. 13–48.

3. Ewart Brookes, *Prologue to a War* (London: White Lion, 1977), passim.

4. Samuel Eliot Morison, *The Two Ocean War* (Boston: Little, Brown, 1963), pp. 272–73.

5. Koburger, *Sea Power*, p. 48–56.

6. Edward P. von der Porten, *The German Navy in World War II* (New York: Thomas Y. Crowell, 1969), p. 27.

1. Italian 12,000-ton V/STOL carrier *Giuseppe Garibaldi*. Note forward ski jump takeoff ramp and Harriers on deck. Courtesy Italian Navy.

2. West German 393-ton 143-class FAC. Armed with two 76-mm guns, four Exocet missiles, and two wire-guided torpedoes. Courtesy FRG Navy.

3: Israeli FACs in column. Gabriel-armed. Craft carry mixed gun types, enabling them to deal collectively with a variety of threats. Courtesy Israeli Navy.

4. U.S. Coast Guard 270-foot cruising cutter. Armed with one 3-inch gun and a helicopter. This ship has not yet broken its commission pennant. Courtesy U.S. Coast Guard.

5. U.S. Coast Guard 110-foot patrol boat. Armed with one 20-mm gun and two 30-cal machine guns. 30-plus knots. Courtesy U.S. Coast Guard.

6. West German 600-ton 206-class submarine. Carries eight torpedoes or twelve to eighteen mines. These boats have numerous near-sisters in foreign fleets. Courtesy FRG Navy.

7. U.S. Navy 136-foot, 215-ton, 12-knot motor minesweeper equipped to sweep moored and influence mines. Courtesy U.S. Naval Institute.

8. U.S. moored contact mines. Note characteristic "horns." Courtesy U.S. Naval Institute.

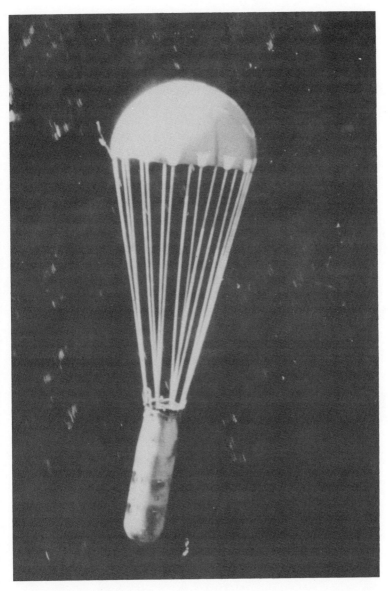

9. U.S. Navy air-dropped influence (magnetic/acoustic) mine. Courtesy U.S. Naval Institute.

10. West German Navy Tornado mach 2.2 shore-based fighter-bomber. Courtesy FRG Navy.

11. U.S. AV-8B V/STOL mach 0.9 fighter-bomber. Developed from British Harrier. Courtesy McDonnel Douglas Corporation.

12. U.S. SH-2D ASW helicopter. Short-range. Armed with sonobuoys, MAD, and ASW torpedoes. Courtesy U.S. Naval Institute.

13. U.S. V-22 tilt-rotor utility plane. Middle-range. Carrier-capable. Courtesy Bell-Boeing.

14. U.S. P-3C land-based, long-range maritime patrol plane, overflying U.S. frigate. Courtesy Lockheed Corporation.

5

The Political Use of Force at Sea

THREAT

The essence of threat is the ability and the will to coerce; to make the object do something it does not want to do, or to refrain from something it wants to do. Threat can be administrative (which does not concern us here) or military—actual, perceived, and/or manufactured. Threat can be direct or indirect, affecting ideology, well-being, or even survival, of course.

Threats at sea can take various carefully graduated armed forms. Ships and planes can be mobilized, crewed, stored, and brought to a war footing. They can be moved to bases near potential objectives, or demonstratively cruise off the other's coast. Threats can result in some form of either compellance or deterrence, in other words, coercion. They do.

Deterrence, achieved through both long- and short-term naval preparation, is a politico-military concept. Through it, one convinces an opponent that any hostile military or naval action would be unprofitable. Involved are fighting effectiveness and according ability to exact an unacceptable penalty, so as sufficiently to raise the political threshold below which any resort to violence is clearly bound to prove too costly.

Compellance, achieved through the same sea-based/sea-related forces, is also a politico-military concept. By it, one convinces an opponent that it would be overwhelmingly easier on him and his interests to do something he does not want to do, than not to do it. Blockade is its most common form, then followed by a warning strike.[1] Compellance is theoretically out of fashion these days.

Even a coast guard's technically internal law enforcement activity can very easily have serious international impact. Witness the three curious so-called cod wars between Iceland and Great Britain, strong case studies of sub-limited low-intensity maritime coercion.

Iceland waged cod wars in 1958–60, 1972–73, and yet once again 1975–76. In each of them, tiny Iceland's tiny coast guard successfully denied mighty Britain's trawlers access to ever-larger fishing areas within its new 200-mile zone. This was a rich area, regularly fished by boats from Hull and Grimsby. For centuries they had come and trawled these waters. But the overall catch was limited in size and henceforward to be reserved for Icelandic boats.

The sturdy trawler-size Icelandic Coast Guard cutters succeeded in this by continually slamming into British fishing boats, and by cutting their trawls, obstructing their work. They similarly harassed the thinner-skinned protecting British frigates. The Icelanders never used their guns. They never had to.

The Icelanders had good political cover. Iceland was otherwise a British ally, and the site of a large strategically located U.S. (NATO) airbase. London's response had to be restrained, in the interest of larger issues.

In any case, there was little opportunity for London to bring its superior military might to bear. If one of the frigates had ever responded by using its guns, the law would have declared this response out of proportion to the delict. Under these conditions, Iceland had to win.

Although we shall come back to this again, limited and sub-limited war swims in a sea of politics. More than ever, Clausewitz' dictum that war is a continuation of diplomacy now with an admixture of other means holds true. The cod wars are an excellent case in point.

REPRISAL

Threats can also take more active military form. When this is less than formally declared war, they are known in law as reprisal. This is the next stage up the escalation ladder. Reprisals are taken in response to a wrongful act, and are characteristically themselves usually small one-time affairs. They supposedly should be appropriate to the delict, proximate in time and place, and generally proportionate to the wrong.

Most likely, a reprisal would start with something selective on the order of a one-time air strike against a single target. Poor response could result in a blockade, or worse.

Properly executed, really large-scale retaliation could severely damage a modern state's civilian economy and strategic potential. Large-scale projection of force could put totally out of action several major ports, and/or a couple of important shipyards, three or four critical coastal power plants, oil production platforms, terminals, and storage tanks, several airfields and rail yards, as well as most if not all merchant shipping and the fishing fleet. It could hit naval vessels and bases, destroying the navy.

In the narrow seas, today, a navy may well have to take positive measures to isolate its reprisal from the activity going on around it. It may well be operating in the midst of considerable neutral traffic. This can become a major politico-military issue, with potentially serious costs. The United States has faced this already.

Exclusion zones may have to be declared. There may be a stationary zone around the target area, providing that any ship or plane found within a given distance of the area will be considered hostile and liable to attack. There may be one or more moving ones surrounding all units of the striking force wherever they may be. Everyone would be warned that any approach that could pose a threat to the force would be dealt with as circumstances dictated, and that all shadowing surface vessels or aircraft would be liable to attack without further ado. These exclusion zones must be widely advertised; there is always someone who does not get the word.

IFF (identification, friend or foe) is always a difficult proposition, in any case. IFF per se uses an electronic challenge-and-response system. It is critical in the narrow seas. In the midst of everything, as two sides clash, there are apt to be fishermen fishing, neutral merchantmen on their occasions, even a third party's men o'war maneuvering close by. There are as apt to be commercial airliners overhead as friendly or hostile warplanes.

IFF assumes that any craft that does not respond properly to a challenge must by default be a foe. But many craft are neither friend nor foe, but neutral. Inevitably, there are equipment malfunctions. Signals may be jammed. Electronic silence may be imposed, closing down IFF along with the rest. IFF positively identifies only friends, and then not all of them.

Foes, neutrals, or even friends may all fail to respond, for one reason or another. Friendlies may not even be aware their IFF equipment is down. To mistake one for the other is a recipe for disaster, no matter which. Yet the challenger has only seconds in which to decide, and to take action on which the survival of his ship may depend.

In those crowded air and surface traffic areas typical of the narrow seas, the only certain answer to this IFF problem seems to be actual physical surveillance, that is, an eyeball check of all intruders either by surface units or by maritime patrol craft flying out far enough to keep any enemy beyond threat (horizon?) distance. Every exclusion zone requires this active support.

Establishment of an exclusion zone is a considerable political as well as military problem. Its radius must be sufficient to create a workable defense area. Yet it cannot for long be so large as to materially hinder normal traffic without stirring up a host of diplomatic costs.

The United States got caught in this trap in the Persian Gulf in 1988, when it shot down an Irani civilian airliner that appeared hostile, overflying one of our cruisers when the ship was in the midst of a skirmish with Irani fast attack craft. The situation should never have been allowed to arise, either by the U.S. force or by the Irani air controllers at Bandar Abbas.

The need for exclusion zones arises as soon as threat response involves the use of force, escalating beyond retorsion to reprisal. The tension between the need for adequate force defense and political necessity will remain until the action is over.

Distant and sporadic blockades have historically been the cause of much ill feeling between belligerent and neutral. A navicert system—developed by the British in WWI—permits the blockader to inspect cargoes at their loading port, verifying their content, origin, and ultimate recipient. This tends to make blockade somewhat more palatable to neutrals. Once a voyage navicert has been issued, dangerous time-consuming open sea visit and search or forced deviation to an inspection port become no longer necessary. Failure to obtain such a certificate opens the ship to all manner of direct and indirect penalty, legal or not.

Thus in the narrow seas today, when traditional surface blockade is instituted, geography and technology together dictate that it be a distant one, preferably established at the sea's access points. Technology has, however, provided a substitute for close blockade—the offensive use of air-laid influence-activated bottom mines.

BLOCKADE UPDATED

In WWII—against Japan—U.S. mining doctrine finally came of age. The United States and its allies laid a total of some 25,000 mines—mostly by air—in Japan's surrounding narrow seas. By the end of the war, Japanese merchant shipping had been all but paralyzed. Over 2,250,000 tons of ships were sunk or damaged by these mines alone, one quarter of the prewar strength of the merchant marine. Lost also were two battleships, two carriers, eight cruisers, thirty-eight destroyers and destroyer escorts, five submarines, and fifty-four other naval vessels.[2]

Korea in 1950 produced an example of the psychological as well as physical impact of mines. Three thousand—contact and influence—hurriedly laid by a scratch flotilla of sampans and junks, denied us the use of North Korea's Wonsan harbor for weeks. These mines effectively delayed our landing and taking over the port for eight days while we gathered information and collected sweepers required to clear first the approaches and then the harbor. There were too few sweepers, too many and too many different types of mines. We lost four sweepers and one tug. Several other ships were damaged. The port was taken by the South Koreans from the land before we ever finished clearing it.

In Vietnam (1965–73), it was not until 1972 that we turned the game around. Eighty-five percent of the war material imported by North Vietnam came in by sea. It was not until we mined the entrances to Haiphong and other northern harbors that the large-scale movement of supplies by sea was cut off. To accomplish this, carrier planes laid some 8000 influence mines, catching twenty-nine large ships in Haiphong alone. Virtually all ships caught inside the ports were immobilized for ten months, and no new shipping entered until the war was over. We ourselves had to clear the mines and open the ports.[3]

Evidently, mines can be laid from almost any platform. Nonetheless, offensive mining today can best be carried out in force by shore-based long-range maritime patrol or bomber aircraft, planes able to deliver sufficient air-laid influence-activated bottom mines. Specifically, the lessons of our recent experience are:

- mining by aircraft in sufficient force can by itself blockade a maritime enemy;

- a few mines cannot long seal a port or close a channel;

- much of the value of a mine effort lies in its surprise introduction and large-scale application before the enemy can organize measures to counter it;

- mining operations must be continuous; fields must be reseeded at frequent intervals, preferably daily;

- effective mining can be obtained through area drops, pinpoint precision is not required;

- if the target area is small, the enemy can and will clear it, at whatever cost;

- a minefield must be dense enough and big enough to ensure that the enemy cannot avoid it;

- as many as ten mines can be dropped before one lands in the right place;
- in shipping channels, one mine per ship/passage is required, perhaps more;
- mining will produce heavy attrition of shipping as a by-product, producing a shipping shortage and clogging repair yards;
- inland waterways can be important mining targets.[4]

THE ROLE OF LAW AT SEA

The history of the international law of the sea is in part and at a certain level the story of a search for workable accommodation between the interests of the coastal (and port) states on the one hand and the generality of sea users (flag states) on the other. Narrow seas tend to be especially affected by this continuing tension, both in peace and war. But there is more to the problem today than that.

Underlying today's aggravated tensions, evident on all sides, are a number of factors. There are small governments staking out new rights on the world map. There are those still working to form a centralized state. Some do not even constitute a single recognized nation. For many of them, having an outside enemy is almost a unifying need. For them, the United States makes an almost perfect "Satan."

Be that as it may, even in the older democratic states governments are under siege. They too are staking out new rights, but are better prepared to recognize the accompanying duties. In these capitals, they are making some effort to reconcile competing interests in some rational kind of way. Witness Western Europe.

Populations are everywhere exploding. Most of this new growth is taking place in the coastal regions, near water-based transportation routes and amenities. Their industrialization and urbanization are proceeding at what have to be previously unheard-of rates. They are all reorganizing not just for survival, but for production. These people all place large new food, fuel, and raw material demands on an already strained international system.

Population growth directly impacts the sea, in a great many ways. Growth drives a mandatory more intensive local exploitation of both inshore and offshore fisheries stocks, within the EEZs and elsewhere. Domestic protein deficits are made up in part by importing fish caught with the permission of or by others. This food must be paid for with exports, which also go by sea.

There is burgeoning exploitation of mineral and energy resources taken from the sea. This brings to the world's have-nots the possibility of previously unimagined riches. These resources are seldom located convenient to those who would use them, and must be transported there by sea. Both shipping and port facilities reflect this.

Inevitably, the seas are having to carry ever-larger pollution loads—industrial wastes, sewage and other urban wastes, agricultural runoff, oil. Narrow seas are particularly vulnerable to pollution, since most contaminants entering their waters tend to remain there, to be continually recirculated in the various basins. This results in stricter user controls, which sometimes unfortunately amount only to a de facto additional tax.

New narrow seas players—and law—steadily appear. At the same time that the world is becoming more interrelated, it is becoming more divided ("Balkanized"). The international system is poorly prepared to handle all this. The system is showing signs of severe strain, nowhere more than on the narrow seas.

Inescapably, the narrow seas see additional new political frictions, of all kinds. Unrestrained—or hardly restrained—competition between would-be sea users results too often in retorsion, reprisal, and even war. Piracy is on the rise again.

How so? Internal to a state, such matters are regulated according to the provisions of its municipal (domestic) law. Laws under these conditions are rules of conduct, adopted by the operative political (sovereign) authority, backed by a usually effective sanction. You should recognize it. It is all around you.

External to a state, no such completed law exists. So-called "international law" is a shambles. International law denotes a body of material presented in treaties, conventions, national constitutions, laws enacted thereunder, and regulations; treatises; and textbooks as a system of rules purporting to regulate the conduct of states.[5] Rules of conduct do abound in this material, but they deal primarily with procedure, little with substance. Few if any are adopted by an interstate political authority. Among nations, enforcement is decentralized to each state. Beyond that, anything not effectively forbidden is permitted.

THE OPERATIONAL ENVIRONMENT

It is a truism to state, today more than ever, that the lifeblood of the Western world moves by sea. Except for a small high-value/low bulk fraction of the total, it is by ship that we move our food, fibers, minerals, manufactured goods, and fuel. Always necessary to the maintenance of our way of life, the protection of those who pass on the narrow seas becomes a matter of survival in times of crisis, sustaining both the West itself and our allies.

The operational environment at such a time will today most probably reflect neither war as traditionally defined, nor peace. Threats of war or reprisal are indeed made; at least partial mobilizations are carried out; isolated outbreaks of violence occur; naval vessels are moved into blockade or raiding positions; merchant shipping steams under increasing conditions of uncertainty, often carrying cargoes considered contraband by one side or the other. The situation can easily escalate into war; or it can just as possibly drift back into another more or less stable local balance of terror. Meanwhile nothing can be allowed that might upset our endless quest for the fragile quiet called "peace."

Territorial seas as such generally now reach out to twelve miles; within these waters a state may freely exercise its sovereign jurisdiction, only limited by law. Contiguous zones—in which a state may continue to exercise fiscal, customs, and sanitary (medical) control—extend to twenty-four miles. EEZs and maritime defense zones both now arbitrarily reach out to 200 miles.

Every vessel has a generally recognized right to unimpeded freedom on the high seas. It can only be boarded by a foreign government there in time of peace if there is prior evidence of piracy, smuggling, or slaving. In time of war, there must be evidence that this is an enemy ship, or that it is a neutral carrying contraband cargo through a blockade.

All violations of law that occur within territorial waters (twelve miles), many of those within contiguous zones (twenty-four miles), and in limited instances those within the EEZs (200 miles) may be prosecuted by the coastal state itself.

Especially in the narrow seas, where interests impinge so closely one on the other, law tends to break down rapidly. Each state becomes its own judge, jury, and enforcer in an ever widening, more troubled area. The situation even encourages and aggravates conflict.

Whatever was hit, it would indicate a threat that if the offending action was not halted forthwith, worse reprisal could yet come. It is not at all certain, however, that this would end the matter, especially with a fanatic, fundamentalist, suicide-hungry, underdeveloped target. Our April 1986 multiple air strikes on Benghazi and Tripoli, in Libya, seriously damaged little of permanent value and may in the long run have had little impact on basic Libyan policy.

Reprisal can lead to counterreprisal, and from there to de facto war. The intention is exactly the opposite, of course. Further escalation is not sought. It may be unavoidable, nonetheless.

DIVISION OF LABOR

When pushed too far, any navy will pull back and concentrate on those tasks considered most essential. This the Royal Navy did twice (1914 and 1939), when challenged by the Germans. Coincident with this is an agreed division of labor, with subsidiary tasks farmed out according to type or area. Allies are found to pick up the slack.

In the spring of 1950, the United States decided to grant military aid to the French fighting in Indochina. The navy members of a joint State-Department of Defense mission sent to survey French needs judged that the objectives of seagoing forces should be as follows:

- to prevent delivery by sea of outside assistance going to the Viet Minh;
- to carry out combined operations against enemy-held coastal regions, including amphibious landings;
- to ensure the flow of supplies to French forces.

Riverine forces were required, too, for the following uses:

- to deny Viet Minh the waterways;
- to interdict enemy logistic traffic;
- to protect French use of the rivers and deltas;
- to enable the French to conduct combined operations there and from there.

The French desired that the U.S. Navy block off Tonkin Gulf and the South China Sea to enemy forces which might come south to attempt landings in support of the Viet Minh, in addition to whatever direct military aid we sent. The blue water tasks were to be for us, the white and brown water ones for the French.

The naval part of the plan worked, to the end. When the French—exhausted—were forced to pull out (1954), the United States simply took over the whole plan.

The relative sensitivity of maritime states to such unfriendly—even hostile—acts at or from the sea can be more or less roughly gauged. An idea of such sensitivity comes from a calculus of several interrelated factors. Rationally, it depends on a state's absolute and relative seagoing trade, merchant marine, shipbuilding, fishing, and other offshore activity, such as oil, gas, and other mineral exploration and production. Also to be considered are such things as strategic position, recent history, alliances, length of coastline, number and location of ports, and offshore zones.

The most sensitive, of course, are islands. Next are those countries with long coastlines and limited land frontiers. Cuba and Italy, respectively, represent these two groups.

The states least sensitive to such actions at sea are, in general, those least developed economically and least populated.

Burma and the Malay countries well represent this group. There are marked exceptions to this, like Saudi Arabia and Kuwait.

BALKANIZATION

The Balkanization of the world has only aggravated a number of endemic maritime problems. Given the sensitivity of most lesser states to anything touching their exercise of absolute sovereignty over their waters, reactions to any attempt to impose limitations on them are often nonrational. Radical and even original interpretations of international law are common. Responsibilities and duties are ignored, rights are stressed. Customary restraints on the use of force are ignored.

In these narrow seas, navies swim in a sea of politics, unstable politics at that. They actively make up their military shortcomings using politics as a tool to even the balance. War is only a continuation of politics, with an admixture of other means.

Demarcation of EEZ boundaries as between adjacent states—especially when offshore islands and narrow seas are involved—is almost always at least a latent source of trouble. There are at least fifty outstanding areas of rival claim worldwide. Although some are now actually in process of settlement, others will arise.

Despite much wishful thinking on the matter, many of the territorial as well as other questions are in the Third World still solved by the direct application of force. In spite of the proliferation of international agencies, war is still the ultimate argument of kings.

In 1969 Irani warships finally escorted an Irani flag merchant ship down from Khorramshahr to the Persian Gulf. Iraq had long held the entire Shatt-al-Arab to be under its sole jurisdiction, and had prevented Irani flag ships from sailing these waters. For lack of a navy, Iran had previously had to give way, but naval action this time secured its purpose. Iran had learned well, as we shall see.

Witness too the seizure by the Turks of Turkish Cyprus, by Iran of the Tunbs in the Persian Gulf, by China and Vietnam of the Paracel and Spratly Islands in the South China Sea, by Indonesia of Portuguese Timor in the southwest Pacific, all as recently as the 1970s. In the more recent 1980s, there was the seizure by Argentina of the Falklands, and their recovery by Britain. Where successful, these all generated or were held to generate offshore zones of great extent and possible riches.

In international law, war is a recognized state of affairs. Wars should be declared, *before* the opening of hostilities. Once a state of war is recognized by the society of nations, the powers divide themselves into two classes—belligerents and neutrals, each with its own rights and duties. In law, neither can be shaded.

There are several generally omitted aspects of all this. In the first place, only states and entities generally recognized as states may declare war. Anyone else committing a warlike act is a terrorist. The duties may be inconvenient, so war declarations are left out.

Neutrals are responsible for preventing the use of their territory as a base by one belligerent for operations against another. Failure to do this deprives them of their status as neutrals. Inability to do so deprives them of the status of state.

In the Third World, conflicts can escalate from retorsion through reprisal to war, or back, nearly instantaneously, much like a summer squall at sea (as happened in the Persian Gulf in 1980). Or it can be an indefinite, interminable process as with the various Arab-Israeli cease-fires. (There has never been peace between Israel and the Arabs; the last cease-fire has at the time of writing been in effect for sixteen years.) It can be full, or partial, only effecting some activities in some areas.

The generally accepted traditional Western definitions common to international law are, therefore, no longer stable, nor understood the same by all. Cease-fire, police action, peace, war, blockade, neutrality, all are terms chosen for an appearance of legality or conciliation, but in reality only to continue to give maximum room within which to pursue one's own ends. They all mean exactly what they are intended to mean at the time. No more, or less.

POLITICIZATION

Finally, a too often forgotten element of all operations out in the narrow seas: Every use of force becomes highly politicized. As the operational equation contains less of the element of overwhelming armed force, it contains more politics. Thus the news contains no objective facts, only items which are possibly dangerous unless and until they are integrated into one highly charged political position or another.

In July 1956, the Egyptian government proclaimed its decision to nationalize the Suez Canal. This led to a full-scale combined British and French amphibious attempt to retake control of the canal by force. The operation was poorly organized and ponderously begun. By the time the landings actually took place—in November—world opinion was being mobilized against them. The most blatant lies were told by the Arabs. When superpower pressure forced the British and French to halt the operation, they were almost in full control of the canal. If they had been just a little quicker, or if they had had just a little more time, they would have had it. Humiliated, the British and French had in any case to withdraw. Nasser had won. He better understood the game.

In 1961, Tunisia had achieved its independence. The large Bizerte naval base complex remained in French hands, however. When finally the Tunisians instituted a blockade of the base to force the French to leave, a small French force made up of a cruiser and two escorts, supported by planes from an off-shore aircraft carrier, broke the blockade, storming into the base. The operation was stillborn, however, politics soon demanding that the ships be pulled back out. The base was eventually given up.

Every military operation out here tends to have its own particular, definite, clearly limited time period within which it must be completed. Otherwise the opposition will be given time to marshal all those political pressures which work against any police action. Witness not only the Suez affair but also the Yom Kippur War (1973) and the Falklands imbroglio (1982). Navies share these politico-military time limits.

Today in the narrow seas, only the fear of reprisal and some occasional public nod to ethics really keep order in international affairs. Objective law has little place. Words have new and twisted meanings. Promises have no value beyond the moment. Only the deed matters.

Since, to be secure, maritime rights and interests have to be protected to the point of sanctions, the necessity for a military maritime force performing police and public service duties is implied, to do just that. At some point, there must also be a war-fighting capability of some size. All along the narrow seas, there is. What do we know about it? What can we know?

Unfortunately, people, arms, money, and propaganda can all too easily be infiltrated to an ally by sea. Raids are all too easily carried out, in said-ally's name. State-sponsored terrorism seems a simple tool with which to harass an enemy. Retribution seems far away.

Conflict potential in Southeast Asia for instance is plainly moving seaward. Maritime disputes in the South China Sea could become the region's next flash point unless the countries involved for once put peace and economic development ahead of an inflexible insistence on rights.

Vietnam, China, and Taiwan maintain rival claims to the Paracel Islands in the South China Sea, which Chinese forces seized in 1974 from Vietnamese troops. The same three nations, along with Malaysia and the Philippines, have claims to the Spratly Islands, south of the Paracels.

All five claimants have armed garrisons on some of the atolls. The Paracels and Spratlys straddle busy shipping lanes, and each island group controls fishing grounds and prospective oil and natural gas under the sea.

As well as asserting jurisdiction over the Paracels and Spratlys, Hanoi has overlapping maritime claims with China in the Gulf of Tonkin, with Indonesia north of the Natuna Islands, and with Malaysia in the Gulf of Thailand. Things do not look good.

CREEPING SOVEREIGNTY AND CLOSED SEAS

Since 1945, the trend in law and practice has been overwhelmingly toward more control by coastal states of the seas off their shores, and by littoral states of their seas. Fueled by a natural-seeming combination of a desire for greater control over their own resources and a need for greater security, the end result has been "creeping sovereignty" and the doctrine of closed seas.

"Creeping sovereignty" extends territorial rights over seabed and subsoil resources from the low water mark beyond the heretofore generally accepted three miles out to the edge of the continental margin; over the fisheries off their shores; over rights of passage, particularly by foreign men o'war, in their coastal and archipelagic waters; and over vessel-source pollution of the water. These rights are carried to the extreme, and often abused, more every day.

Closed seas denies the right of any man o'war other than those flying the flag of a riparian state to enter that particular body of water. Sometimes the claim is only partial, to restrict the number or type, or the weapons they can carry, or the length of their stay. Application of this doctrine denies outsiders protection for their trade or any other political use of force. The Black and Baltic Seas see this from time to time.

Narrow seas having more than one littoral state, but dominated by one of them, will see vigorous attempts by that state to declare and have accepted that sea as a neutral "zone of peace," or nuclear-free sea, or some such. This in effect turns those waters into a closed sea, working to keep extraregional powers out, and legitimizing domination by the stronger regional state.[6]

If any of these moves succeeds—proposals keep popping up—that sea's lesser rim states tend to come completely within the naval orbit of the stronger one. Whatever maritime independence they had enjoyed by playing between the big powers is usually gone.

Should a hostile state gain or hold control of the entrance(s) to their sea, able to block or destroy it, closing off through trade, that state gains an important weapon against any extraregional power as well as against any local one. Even if weaker, it can choke off the maritime trade of the dominant state at will. Those entrance(s) are key. Witness Turkey at the Bosphorous/Dardanelles, the entrance to the Black Sea. Think of Oman and Iran at Hormuz. These places lock up the world.

CONFLICT

Littoral powers (coastal and port states) have three broad peacetime rights and responsibilities off their coasts: sovereignty, jurisdiction, and recognized control; good order, including control of such diverse elements as navigation, piracy, ship-source pollution, and waste disposal; and resource (fish, oil and gas, sand and gravel, minerals) use.

In wartime, to these, littoral states must add "sea control," or at least "sea denial," to defend all of the above.

Few of the smaller states achieve all of these, measured either against extraregional outsiders or even their neighbors, except in Western Europe. Canada, Israel, South Africa, India, Australia, and Japan also do a good job.

Nonlittoral powers (flag states) also have three broad peacetime interests in the narrow seas: through passage, inshore as well as offshore; access to local ports for refuge and trade; and legitimate (licensed?) resource use (fishing, oil and gas exploitation, mining). In wartime, to these must be added "sea control" and "projection of power." None of this is automatic any more. They seldom were.

Territorial seas are normally subject to two different passage regimes. There is a long-standing general legal regime, historically based on commercial convenience—the right of innocent passage, applying to merchant shipping. This innocent passage is suspendible, does not allow automatic overflight by aircraft, and forbids submerged passage of submarines at any time. International straits, however, are now subject to transit passage—a nonsuspendible right, allowing both overflight above and submerged passage below. Specific "historic" straits like the Skagerrak and the Kattegat are excepted, being allowed to continue to apply the old rules.

Fishermen are notoriously independent souls, normally following the fish wherever they go. Fishermen will catch, clean, and ice down anything saleable they can get their hands on. From prehistory, they have been, are, and will be the cause of many clashes of interest between states.

In the narrow seas, then, the political world is today in general highly unstable. Nation-states and would-be nation-states push, elbow, and shove, each on its own. The role of law at sea is a poor one, each state being its own law. Here in the narrow seas at least, the state thus continues its primacy in international affairs. The state watches over the survival and well-being of its people, and pushes its ideology. States fight to preserve their identity (independence and territorial integrity) and to create and maintain conditions in which their interests (way of life) can flourish. In the narrow seas, it is their largely unfettered writ which.runs.

A *maritime state* is thus one whose vital interests are primarily sea-related or can be secured by mostly maritime means. It will be numbered among the coastal and port or small flag states. It will have a merchant and fishing fleet of some size. Under newly accepted law, with EEZs the average coastal state will have increased its marine domain by about 1600 percent. It will be an active player on the international scene. It will have a navy, almost certainly a small one, with which to defend itself and further its interests at sea. Mostly, it borders a narrow sea.

The United States is a maritime state, too.

NOTES

1. Edward N. Luttwak, *The Political Uses of Sea Power* (Baltimore, MD: Johns Hopkins University Press, 1974), pp. 24–38.

2. Johnson and Katcher, *Mines Against Japan* (White Oak, MD: Naval Ordnance Laboratory, 1973), pp. 29–30.

3. Maurice Griffiths, *The Hidden Menace* (Greenwich: Conway Maritime Press, 1981), p. 127.

4. Johnson and Katcher, p. 134.

5. Percy Elwood Corbett, *The Study of International Law*. Short Studies in Political Science (Garden City, NY: Doubleday, 1955), pp. 2–7.

6. James Cable, "The Freedom of the Baltic," *Navy International* (May 1989): 225–27.

6

The Persian Gulf

THE SETTING

Far off across the world, the hot, sun-blasted waters of the Persian—or Arabian—Gulf are today seemingly alive with merchant shipping, en route to or from one or more of the gulf's many modern oil-loading terminals or new commercial ports. The many fishermen only add to the scene. Most vessels carry one of the many flags of the Free World, of bordering Arab states, or of Iran, engaged upon their lawful occasions. The gulf is a busy place.

On a normal day, one oil tanker passes either into the gulf to be loaded, or out, gorged with as much as 100,000 to 500,000 tons of black gold, on the average of every thirty minutes, all day, every day, fueling the industrial world. To this may be added other extremely heavy cargo traffic—large, fast container ships; break-bulk freighters; bulk carriers and the like—on which no specific count appears to be available, as well as the many colorful local craft.

The briefest politico-economic survey shows that from the gulf comes some 40 percent of the Free World's oil, or 60 percent of all the oil flowing in international trade. This includes two-thirds of the petroleum energy requirements of Western Europe and 80 percent of Japan's. The only way all this oil can be paid for is through trade, the export to the gulf of food, fibers, minerals, and manufactures. The *only* way to move either the oil or the goods with which to pay for it is by ship. The very viability of the Gulf States—which must import almost everything except oil—depends on the maintenance of this international traffic, as well as on protection of the extensive largely dhow-borne intraregional trade. This shipping is important to all the world.

Accordingly, the United States has since the 1940s maintained a permanent naval presence in the gulf—the Middle East Force, normally a headquarters ship and from two to four destroyers and frigates—informally based at Bahrain. It is still there, having been heavily augmented during the 1980s and now drawn down again. It had in the meantime been through a major exercise of war in the narrow seas.

THE IRAN-IRAQ WAR

The bitter eight-year Iran-Iraq Persian Gulf War offers us an excellent example of war in the narrow seas. The Iran-Iraq war, which began in 1980, had claimed, by the time it ended in 1988, roughly 600 merchantmen damaged or sunk, victims of attack from the air by both sides or Irani mines. Some seventy-five merchantmen caught at the outbreak in the Shatt-al-Arab were abandoned, constructive total losses.

Insurance rates for ships going to the Irani commercial port of Bandar Khomaini at the head of the Persian Gulf were soon quoted as 20 percent of hull value. They were 7.5 percent for ships headed to its oil terminal Kharg Island, eighty miles southeast. Traffic continued, nonetheless.

The gulf war's antishipping operations might be described as an exceptionally crude form of blockade and counterblockade.

Although the much superior Irani Navy (see Table 2) had wiped out the Iraqi surface fleet almost at once, and commanded the gulf entrance, the Iraqis—relying on their air superiority—could still have fully denied the sea to the Iranis.

Table 2
Irani Navy, 1980–81

Ships:	3 guided missile destroyers
	8 frigates
	9 FACs (missile armed)
	5 mine warfare ships
	4 amphibious warfare ships
	14 ACVs
	assorted patrol boats
	assorted auxiliaries
Planes:	35 helicopters
	6 maritime patrol aircraft
	10 transports
Bases:	4 (Bandar Abbas - main base;
	Khorramshar;
	Kharg Island;
	Chah Bahar)

Some of the ships and planes may have been lost or damaged in the early fighting, or have been laid up for lack of parts.

Source: Jean Labayle Couhat, ed.; A. D. Baker III, trans.; *Combat Fleets of the World 1980–81* (Annapolis: Naval Institute Press, 1980), pp. 270–76.

Iran's vital oil exports and arms imports could have been closed down at any time. Refueled in the air from Arab bases, Iraq's planes were capable of dominating the entire 500-mile long gulf, occasionally to outside the Strait of Hormuz.

The Iranis—although seriously deficient in air power—still retained a surface fleet sufficient to prevent all oil exports on Iraqi flag tankers. Complete sea control, however, was beyond them, except at the entrance to the gulf.

Teheran nonetheless announced that if it could not use the gulf to move its cargoes, neither would anyone else. Irani mining followed, even off Khor Fakkan, outside the gulf in the United Arab Emirates. So did harassing by fast attack craft.

Irani missiles were fired at Kuwait's tanker anchorage through which Iraqi oil still moved.

Neither Teheran nor Baghdad ever took the naval war to its logical conclusion. Instead, there was a typical Near and Middle Eastern compromise, for which the United States paid. The experience encapsulizes conflict in the Third World today.

THE BRIDGETON CONVOY

In late July 1987 five ships departed Khor Fakkan—a small U.A.E. port fifty-five miles south of and outside the Strait of Hormuz—for Kuwait, 600 miles away through the strait and up the length of the Persian Gulf. This was the first U.S. Navy–escorted convoy of the first two recently U.S.-reflagged Kuwaiti tankers, but no one expected any trouble the strong anti-air and -surface escorts could not handle. The escorts' sea and anchor details were called away, and cables hauled short. Once underway, the convoy formed up. First came USS *Fox*, guided missile cruiser, carrying the escort group's senior officer. This was followed by U.S. flag supertanker *Bridgeton*, LPG carrier *Gas Prince*, frigate USS *Crommelin*, and destroyer USS *Kidd*, in that order.

As the ships moved north, their crews went to general quarters, ready to pass through the strait, considered to be the most dangerous segment of the passage. The fifty-mile-long strait was guarded by Chinese-built Silkworm coast defense surface-to-surface missiles located on Queshm Island at the head of the bend, and just to the east of it, on the mainland. Their sites had been pinpointed, and their distinctive radar signature heard. Irani airfields were nearby, on Lavan Island and at Bandar Abbas, covering the strait. The multitude of abandoned oil and gas rigs just inside the mouth were known bases both for the speedboats and for the helicopters that threatened passing ships.

In the event, however, the convoy and its escorts passed through the strait without incident. The five ships continued northwest, to Kuwait at the very head of the gulf. Crews began to breathe a little easier. At a steady sixteen knots, the ships ploughed steadily up the deep draft channel, a one-mile interval between them.

Then just after dawn the following day, twenty miles west of Farsi Island, the unthinkable took place. Through the already one hundred degree heat came the sound of an explosion. *Bridgeton* had hit a mine, blowing open four of her tanks. Only a small delay was imposed on the convoy, but the gulf (and the world) was then treated to the spectacle of the damaged tanker leading the naval escort and *Gas Prince* in through the last 120 miles, the others following carefully in single line ahead. A strong blow had just been struck to the United States' political and military prestige.

BACKGROUND POLITICS

Mesopotamia has always been a battleground between Persian and Arab. Baghdad dates the latest war from September 4, 1980, when Irani guns first shelled Iraqi border villages during a long-standing dispute over the Shatt-al-Arab. Teheran dates the start as the twenty-second, marking Iraq's first open crossing of the border. The enmity between them was thus fundamental, just sharpened up and become unusually vicious.

Loyalties in general are long established out there, largely based on geographic position and on trading patterns. Although more than most areas, the gulf basin forms a cultural whole—even with Sunni Arabs on one side and Shiite Iranis on the other—there are both fundamental and subtle differences between all the various political entities.

With a reputation as a warrior state, richer and more populous than the other Arab Gulf states, Iraq vies with Egypt and Syria for leadership of the modern Arab world. Neighboring Kuwait looks to Iraq for support. The tiny emirates making up the U.A.E. far away in the southern gulf have to look to each other. So do Bahrain and Qatar in the center, although less so; they have Saudi Arabia to help. Oman at the Strait of Hormuz, at the mouth, having actively if quietly thrown its lot in with the West some time ago, is the exception—not the rule.

Especially in the southern gulf, Iran's overall position as regional superpower neighbor to the small Arab coastal city-states becomes quite clear. Both the Arabs and the Iranis—historically trapped in the gulf basin by the mountain and desert barriers behind them—have taken the line of least resistance and developed their commerce (and the inevitably accompanying cultural ties) using the sea.

The Arabs of the "trucial coast" were famous as navigators, traders, pearl fishermen, smugglers, slavers, and pirates. Today some newly rich from oil (Dubai and Abu Dhabi), some with a long trading relationship with Iran, all acutely aware of their large neighbor across the water, they have to tread the most carefully, war or no war.

Dubai, for instance, also the quintessential trading entrepot, still maintained a very lucrative trade to and from Iran. Sharjah and Iran still share oil production facilities on the nearby island of Abu Musa. Here on the gulf's southern rim, survival has long depended on skillful maneuver, diplomacy, and, ultimately, accommodation with Iran, not on force.

KUWAIT AND THE UNITED STATES

As a matter of record, none of the Gulf States had been enthusiastic about a Great Power presence there. Any presence. Not since the Shah of Iran fell, at any rate. They have always felt that their fundamental community of interest was strong enough to weather any quarrel of the moment. Most excesses of force were avoided, and settlements kept limited. The rulers generally agreed on one thing, at least: They did not want to import the Great Power conflict to the area. Some of the states carefully restricted their cooperation because they knew they would have to live with whatever situation was left them after the outside powers went back home.

Kuwait—Iraq's benevolently neutral, rich little neighbor—began this particular maritime crisis by quietly opening its commercial port to receipt of war material destined for Baghdad, and its oil terminal to the export of oil for Iraqi account. Increasingly feeling threatened by the resulting Irani pressure, Kuwait moved in December 1986 to internationalize the war, in the name of freedom of the seas. Kuwait appealed to the United States, the Soviet Union, China, and others for help. Enthusiasm among the Arabs—especially those of the south— was somewhat less than universal, but the move was made.

In late February 1987, the Soviet Union responded to Kuwait's request by chartering three of its own tankers to the little state. Apparently caught off guard, it was the next month before Washington finally agreed to reflag eleven Kuwaiti tankers. The first two took part in the July convoy.

Concurrently, Kuwait received an offer of naval protection from Moscow. This was reduced to escort of Russian ships. We agreed to escort of our own, ensuring their safe and timely arrival, as part of the deal.

Also in response to increasingly angry Irani pressure, Kuwait had taken to shuttling oil out of the gulf in its own large tankers, for later sale. *Bridgeton*—1200 feet long, displacing 401,400 tons—was intended for this service. The shuttle tankers moor off Khor Fakkan, acting as floating storage as long as required, transferring cargo to smaller customers on call. This helped keep insurance rates down, too.

THE THREAT—BLOCKADE

The overall basic naval threat to merchant shipping in the gulf took various forms over the years, shifting with the situation. There was an announced blockade, inevitably an incomplete "paper" one, established by Iran, of all cargoes for Iraq and military cargoes to Kuwait. Iranian naval vessels operated primarily around the Strait of Hormuz, the gulf entrance shipping lane choke point, intermittently exercising a legitimate belligerent right of stopping, boarding, searching, and sometimes seizing ships. Vessels were stopped, some were forced into Bandar Abbas. In a few cases, cargoes were seized (contraband war material destined for Iraq, of course). Shots were even fired across bows.

It was this which led to the large-scale appearance of Great Power warships in the gulf, either expanding a token earlier force (American), reinstituting an earlier presence (British), or initiating a new one (French). These men o'war convoyed ships carrying their flags, interposed themselves to prevent Iranian challenges, visits and searches, or other hostile acts. The Soviets—newly arrived—acted the same. They did, nonetheless, play their own game.

In reaction to the increasing violence that accompanied the bitter Irani blockade, the British Royal Navy had gradually built up its Armilla patrol—one support ship and a few escort types—stationed just outside the Strait of Hormuz. To these were added a number of minesweepers, as their need became clear.

At the height of the crisis, the French Navy deployed a small carrier task group to the Arabian Sea, outside the Persian Gulf, along with six mine countermeasure vessels. The carrier task group remained for some fourteen months outside the strait. The sweepers went in.

Even the British and French, nonetheless, held back—technically in any case. Officially, these two accompanied ("shadowed")—they did not escort—their ships through the blockade. Neither London nor Paris wished to become any more involved here—or to be seen to be involved—than they had to be.

London and Paris, therefore, established and maintained this legal fiction. In an escort, the navy leads the way and picks the route. In accompaniment, the warship steams close by while the merchantman picks the route. Nonetheless, the groups often took on the de facto aspects of a convoy.

Prudence, therefore, dictated some alteration in the normal scheme of things, in any case. One result was that arriving merchantmen took to sending a portion of their crews ashore—those not absolutely necessary simply to drive the ship—at Khor Fakkan or elsewhere outside the Strait of Hormuz, to be picked up again on the way out. Other measures were also being taken, as we shall see.

THE THREAT—SURFACE ATTACKS

Attack by or from Iranian surface ships and craft employing guns, missiles, or even boarders offered the most likely threat here to be faced by the merchantmen. In type these vessels ran the full gamut of technical complexity, extending from decrepit native fishing boats and dhows to the full range of minor men o'war. Their employment is familiar; base facilities already existed or could be easily improvised about anywhere. Crews could always be had.

Iran's quasi-military Revolutionary Guards (the Pasdaran—religious zealots) converted an order of forty–fifty Swedish-built speedboats to hit-and-run attack craft. Produced by Boghammer Marin Company, these aluminum boats are roughly 42 feet long, and are driven by twin 305-horsepower diesel engines. Reportedly this gave them a cruising speed of forty knots and a sprint capability of sixty knots. Armed locally with recoilless rifles, machine guns, and hand-held rocket-propelled grenades, these boats have a range of 500 more than adequate nautical miles. Based in the Sirri-Abu Musa Islands in the lower gulf and at Farsi Island in the northern, as well as at the ubiquitous oil platforms, they constituted one of the three major threats to passing traffic.

These "Boghammers" were sometimes transported on board Irani naval landing ships, those equipped with a helicopter deck and the necessary crane. In these instances, the helicopter carried on board was used to locate potential targets. The crane was used to lower and recover the boats. One common tactic was to loiter behind a screen of fishing boats, and then to pounce upon the quarry when it neared.

The Pasdaran characteristically approached without warning, let loose a barrage of fire, then sped away. They tended to attack during darkness or at first light, sometimes shooting up a target for as long as twenty minutes before taking off.

Such random—almost indiscriminate—terrorism was not typical of Iran's regular forces, however. Ordinarily, Irani long-range maritime patrol craft—navy-manned—would overfly unidentified ships. Then, between one and three hours later, the ships could expect to be stopped and visited. (The delay strongly indicated a requirement to obtain approval from shore.)

Irani military helos and fixed-wing aircraft always sought to follow international blockade law, identifying a vessel's flag and cargo before taking any action. Clearance to continue a voyage was often granted by radio.

Boghammers having become the threat they were, armed

suppression began. In early July, the Iraqis carried out several air raids on Sirri and Farsi and on oil platforms known to be speedboat bases. Since they could operate from almost any shallow bay or cove, or from "mother ships" undistinguishable from the rest of the always considerable local traffic (that specifically included fishing boats and dhows), the Boghammers were never entirely put down.

THE THREAT—MINES

Although they might have been the most visible, fast hit-and-run attack boats were not the only menace faced out there. Next after these craft in importance came Iran's mines. Bottom, floating, or moored; contact, influence (magnetic, acoustic, and/or pressure), or controlled, mines are simple, rugged weapons. Cheap, too. They could be laid from almost any fishing boat or dhow. They could be time-delayed, ship-counting, or immediately armed.

Earlier that year, in May, some dozen old but effective North Korean–manufactured MO8[1] moored contact mines of WWI Anglo-Russian design laid by Iran were cleared from the entrance to Kuwait's Mina al Ahmadi oil terminal. Each MO8 contained a 250-pound explosive load. Before mine clearance was complete, four tankers—including one Russian—were damaged. We had been warned.

Then in July, one of two ships in the very first inbound convoy of U.S. reflagged Kuwaiti tankers was mined. U.S. intelligence had detected Irani activity in the region of Farsi Island— one of the deep draft channel's choke points—during the night of 23–24 July, as the *Bridgeton* convoy neared. But for whatever reasons, naval planners attached a low probability to any mine threat in the open waters of the gulf. No action was taken.

It was another MO8 that damaged *Bridgeton*, but due to its inherent bulk, compartmentalization, and strong scantlings, the tanker was able to complete its passage in without help. The MO8 would probably have sunk any one of the smaller and lighter escorts. Several days later, mine clearance teams discovered that the Farsi Island field contained at least seven more of the MO8s. Nothing more sophisticated was ever seen.

In its mine plan, however, if there was one, Teheran gave up one essential of success: surprise. It frittered away its mine stocks in sequential minor efforts. The mines remained primarily a nuisance, never overwhelming the sweepers, never closing the shipping lanes, mostly swept one way or another by whatever means was at hand. Had the Iranis laid more mines, all at once, using every means, and kept doing it, the final outcome might have been different than it was.

THE THREAT—MISSILES

The effective Irani missile threat was very real but confined largely to two types: large Silkworm surface-to-surface and small helicopter-launched air-to-surface weapons. Short of flyable fixed-wing high performance strike aircraft, they employed their helicopters in an antiship role. Basing these helos on pads along the coast, and on oil rigs, they armed them with French-built AS-12 light antiship missiles. The AS-12 had a range of 10,000 yards, guided manually using line-of-sight wire. The AS-12 had the punch of a 6-inch shell.

Those of Iran's few remaining operational U.S.-built F-4 Phantom fighters based on Lavan still constituted a threat; they were equipped with 15-mile-range TV-guided Maverick air-to-surface missiles. They were few, and in the event not used. They would have done heavier damage.

Iran still disposed of a number of missile frigates armed with Italian Sea Killer surface-to-surface missiles. These too had to be reckoned with, to the end.

Last but not least came the Chinese-designed Silkworm coast defense missiles. Some dozen appeared to be sited on Queshm Island and more on the mainland to the east, on the northern side of the critical Strait of Hormuz. There were additional sites at the head of the gulf, probably protecting Bandar Khomaini (the major commercial port) and other facilities up there.

Cousins of the Soviet Styx, Silkworms have an operational range of fifty miles, more than enough to cover the Hormuz strait. These missiles were semimobile, and could be brought operational on very short notice. They were never fired at us.[2] They gave another name to the Strait of Hormuz, which became also known as "Silkworm Alley" in deference to the missiles' half-ton warhead.

THE BEGINNING OF THE END?

On July 20, 1987, the U.N. Security Council unanimously passed a resolution (No. 598) demanding a cease-fire between Iran and Iraq. Concurrently there was to be an exchange of prisoners held by both sides and withdrawal to original borders pending final settlement of the war. Iraq accepted 598 in its entirety at once, and halted its attacks on gulf (Irani) shipping.

Iran never officially accepted nor rejected the U.N. demand, working to turn it to its politico-military tactical advantage. Teheran continued its attacks on merchant shipping, and its mining. It went through the motions of negotiating conditions, continuing its own impossible demands. Patently stalling for time, meanwhile furiously selling oil, Iran allowed six weeks to pass. No concrete progress was made.

Then on August 29, its patience exhausted, Iraq renewed its air attacks on Irani shipping, terminals, and bases. In a massive effort, its planes struck oil-loading facilities at Sirri and Lavan, a tanker at Sirri, and a platform in the Rakhsh oil field (all in the southern gulf); the naval base on Farsi Island and a tanker in the northern gulf, all on the same day. Kharg was hit the following day. The de facto Iraqi Gulf shipping truce had ended. A new phase of the war was beginning. Iran promised it would be a lively one. It was. Lloyd's raised its base rate 50 percent on hulls.

Attacks by Iraq on gulf merchant shipping had begun in 1981, those by Iran in 1984. By 1986, between them they were hitting over a hundred ships a year. In 1987, the total was a little under 200. In 1988—up to August 20—they attacked some ninety, if one pro rates the figures, about the same number (see Table 3).

Table 3
Attacks on Ships in the Persian Gulf Region, by Belligerent, 1981-88

Attacker	1981	1982	1983	1984	1985	1986	1987	1988*	Total
Iraq	5	22	16	53	33	66	89	38	322
Iran	0	0	0	18	14	45	92	52	221
Total	5	22	16	71	47	111	181	90	543

Source: Ronald O'Rourke, "Gulf Ops," *U.S. Naval Institute Proceedings,* (May 1989), p. 43. Reprinted from *Proceedings* with permission; Copyright © (1988) U.S. Naval Institute.
*Cease-fire went into effect 20 August 1988.

By 1988, escorted and accompanied merchantmen were successfully getting through. It was the independents and flags of convenience that were getting hit. Some began to tag along with the convoys. Often, special gulf passage crews were placed on board, and the regular crews taken off. They hosed down their stacks to keep them cool. Crews improvised anti-flash gear—hard hats, industrial protective glasses, and the like.

If necessary, the world could do without Iran's oil. Its contribution could easily be made up through more production from others. The world could not, however, long do without that of the gulf as a whole.

As the situation worked out, it was Western seapower that guaranteed once again that the shipping lanes would carry enough to meet the world's minimum requirements, at least. That reluctant sea dragon—the United States—led the way. The outcome those who read this know: In August 1988—a year later—a cease-fire was finally agreed upon. Peace is not yet.

THE UNITED STATES IN THE MAZE

From the naval point of view, clearly, the most effective, least destructive, even easiest way for the United States in 1988 to put pressure on Iran to make peace would have been to institute a traditional blockade of Irani oil exports. Established well outside the Strait of Hormuz, perhaps in the name of the United Nations, blockading ships could have halted all tankers carrying Irani oil and held them until Teheran accepted and acted on Resolution 598. Reprisals could easily have been taken for any Irani action against the blockading force.

At one stroke, we would entirely cut off Iran's oil money. No money, no replenishment arms or ammunition. No new arms, soon no war. Fighting through our own convoys could have continued meanwhile, if it was considered really necessary to run them in the interim.

But many in the industrialized world depended heavily on the free flow of Irani oil, especially the Japanese. Even more relied on gulf oil as a whole. Teheran had made its position very clear—if it could not ship oil out, nobody in the gulf would. Torching the gulf's oil fields would not have been beyond it. Politics therefore demanded that other less satisfactory means (diplomacy, embargo) had first to be tried.

In May 1987, Middle East Force's USS *Stark* (FFG-31) was attacked apparently unintentionally by an Iraqi aircraft while on radar picket station in the central gulf. *Stark* was hit by two Exocet missiles; thirty-seven U.S. sailors were killed. The ship was saved. There was no retaliation, although strong measures to improve IFF were taken on both sides. We were now ready for serious work.

As the United States built up its forces in the gulf, we depended on a number of things only the Arabs could provide: base rights for our planes; port access for our ships; limited joint military planning; even occasional military cooperation. Saudi Arabia–based planes surveilled the battle area. Tiny Bahrain had long granted facilities to the navy's Middle East Task Force. Oman did the same. Increasingly, the others helped in various ways, some even fueling our ships. It was, after all, their war as well as ours.

Outside the gulf, the United States soon assembled a supercarrier (at one point there were two), a battleship, and a battalion of marines, along with appropriate escorts. Its smaller ships were steadily rotated into the gulf, taking the place of those long enough there.

Inside the gulf, the United States eventually assembled a patrol and escort force of some thirty ships and craft, including a 39,000-ton V/STOL carrier (normally a marine helicopter assault ship) at the top end of the spectrum, and minesweeping boats on the other. With the many aircraft and special units, it was the largest buildup since the Vietnam War.

The gulf itself was divided into sectors, each sector being permanently patrolled. Convoys were still escorted, passing through the sectors, up or down.

A large civilian crane barge was acquired, pushed out to a position three miles west of Farsi Island, and anchored there as an advanced patrol craft base. On it were stationed several borrowed army night attack helos, which worked with our patrol boats. Boats were lifted aboard for heavy maintenance. Crews were berthed there. Irani activities on Farsi—under close surveillance—were checkmated.

In Washington, the navy instituted a request for some few of the Coast Guard's 110-foot patrol boats, for gulf service. With additional armament, these would have made first-rate Boghammer killers. It was, however, ultimately decided that the guard's domestic tasks—the drug war—precluded their then being diverted to such duty.

To manage its escalating military presence, the United States created a special joint Persian Gulf operational headquarters. The joint force commander—a navy admiral—had overall cognizance of regional military activities. He reported to the Joint Chiefs of Staff. He flew his flag first on the supercarrier, then on command ship *Lasalle*, inside the gulf. We were there to stay.

In April 1988, USS *Samuel B. Roberts* (FFG-58) steamed into a minefield while on patrol in the central gulf, near Rostam and the Shah Allum Shoal. *Roberts* hit one of the mines while maneuvering to avoid others, and was almost cut in two. Ten crewmen were injured, some seriously. The ship was saved.

In response to this and other unfriendly acts, reprisals were taken: one Irani minelayer (*Iran Ajr*), a frigate (*Sahand*), and a patrol boat (*Joshan*) were captured and/or sunk, and a number of oil rigs were shot up. Frigate *Sabalan* was severely damaged. But the military and political damage had been done. There was no marked reaction from Iran.

Intermittent hostilities continued, U.S. flag ships being escorted and sometimes attacked, the navy occasionally retaliating. Then in July 1988, an Irani civilian airliner out of Bandar Abbas en route Dubai overflew U.S. missile cruiser *Vincennes* during a surface firefight, and was shot down. All 290 passengers and crew were killed. Although this was undoubtedly a mistake—albeit a tragic one—it will never be possible to convince the Iranis of that.

U.S. operations in the gulf during these two years are typical of low intensity maritime warfare conducted in a politically constrained environment. It was always what did not happen that really mattered. If we had not intervened, Iran would sooner or later have closed down all gulf oil traffic except its own. This we managed to prevent. So far we have, at least.

As should by now be clear, the gulf's physical environment is a harsh one. Ships must cool their machinery with sea water that can run fifty degrees hotter than that they normally use. The hotter the air is, the less helicopters can lift. Those frequent dust storms create major maintenance problems. Grit gets into everything. Moving surfaces wear fast. The stay is not an easy one, at best.

U.S. ANTIMINE POLICY

The United States traditionally has to a large extent depended on allies with greater minesweeping capabilities to carry that common burden. There has in NATO thus been a natural division of labor. With, in any case, greater resources, the United States has built and operated the super-carriers, the battleships, and the various other large strike elements of the alliance's naval forces. The Western European navies—having to keep open their waters to receive wartime reinforcement and resupply, no matter what—concentrate on ASW and minesweeping, more directly of concern to them.

The United States' own antimine capability, while certainly not non existent, has therefore definitely been a limited one. Thus we in the 1980s manned a mere half dozen aging Korean War-era surface minesweepers. Only three of these, however, had active duty crews. All six eventually ended up in the gulf, contributing what they could.

By the opening of 1988, U.S. ships on station in the gulf were being joined by the independently operating British and French sweepers mentioned earlier, as well as by Italian, Belgian, and Dutch units. For reason of their individual domestic politics, however, whatever coordination of effort between U.S. and European units there was, was effected unofficially by the commanding officers on scene.

Although a new class of U.S. surface sweepers was on its involved way through the authorization, design, building, and working up process, and had been for a while, even the lead ship was a long way from being operationally ready.

Anyway, the United States had developed and preferred to use a unique high tech system, using large helicopters each towing an instrumented minesweeping sled for most mine detection and subsequent clearance. There were perhaps only two dozen of these RH53D Sea Stallion helo and sled teams. Unfortunately, too, their mission profiles ran at most to three and-a-half hours each. The technique had been well developed, however, having been employed to help clear the Suez Canal in the mid-1970s, after the Yom Kippur War.

As one result of the *Bridgeton* convoy, eight of our meager pool of minesweeping helos were loaded on C5A Galaxy transports and flown from the United States to Diego Garcia. There they were taken aboard the V/STOL carrier, which became their base. They regularly worked inside the Persian Gulf.

International naval cooperation proved essential if the gulf was to be cleared for traffic. Cooperation there was, locally at least. Mines were swept. Basic U.S. policy had to be working again. Barely. But enough.

ALLIED HELP

Bridgeton's July 1987 mining led to immediate U.S. requests to its European NATO allies for mine countermeasure vessels to operate under U.S. command in the gulf. To this there was no response, and no European ships ever came under its control. But the allies did concert a gulf presence of their own, within the limits of their various politics.

In August, Iran moved its mining offensive 500 miles out beyond the Strait of Hormuz to the busy waters of al Fujairah. Tanker *Texaco Caribbean* was holed and more mines were spotted. That did it.

The British sent four countermeasure ships, accompanied by a support and a repair ship, joining the escort force already on scene. France added three sweepers to its area forces. Benelux (the Netherlands and Belgium) and then the Italians joined soon after. These contingents remained national forces under national command, however.

On scene commanders kept each other informed in advance of tactical and technical matters such as ship movements, mine countermeasure operations, and port visits. After one initial fiasco clearly demonstrated that to accomplish their tasks they *had* to work together, things got better.

When *Samuel B. Roberts* hit a mine in an area previously declared secure, the Benelux force, the British and the Italians did the mine hunting and clearing. Local commanders—U.S. ones included—further integrated their various activities, standardizing mine reporting procedures. Three "areas of interest" were designated, stretching from Qatar to Hormuz. The intention was now to have at least one command unit and three mine countermeasure ships available in each of them.

After the cease-fire, there was a high level meeting in London which organized joint mine clearance along the principal shipping routes in the lower gulf. Once again, however, the task was carried out by individual forces under existing national command.

Significantly more could have been achieved by the Europeans in the Gulf given fewer political constraints on all sides. It would have taken, for instance, only half the ships—properly coordinated—to have done the same job. This time we were able to pay the price. Next time . . .

NOTES

1. Each MO8 assembly (mine, anchor, cable) weighed about half a ton. The sail and motor-driven local craft could each carry up to three of them.

2. With one possible reported exception—diverted by decoys—they were not fired in their coast defense role, in any case. Nor by extension in a waterway denial role. Firing from map coordinates and allowing terminal homing to do the rest, the Iranis did hit stationary targets in Kuwaiti anchorages, to some effect. Mina al Ahmadi oil terminal had to be closed down temporarily, but was soon reopened, as the missiles' land base fell to the Iraqis.

7

Conclusion

LANDFALL?

Navies today tend to divide themselves into three groups: super-navies (the United States and the Soviet Union); medium navies, if we have to separate them; and the lesser others. The super-navies have world-class status. The medium navies are those smaller navies of strong regional value. The others are primarily of local worth. It is primarily these last which we are looking at here, and their impact on us.

Seapower is the military ability to influence events on the sea and from the sea. Components are ships, planes, men, and bases, organized into a headquarters, shore facilities, and operating forces. Enough of the right kind of seapower for the time and place gives command of the sea, in classic terms the ability to use the sea for one's own ends, and to deny this to others.

Most naval thought is Mahanian, or post-Mahan. It is written for large blue water high seas navies vying for command of the sea during the first half of the twentieth century. The big gun ship, the decisive battle, total blockade, the fleet in being, convoy, all these concepts are familiar to us. This is *naval* war.

Third World conflicts do not appear against this familiar, established backdrop. With changed conditions, terms are redefined. Although the jargon is recognizable, the terms used in individual situations mean exactly what they are intended to mean at the time by the person using them. Think the worst.

Today in the narrow seas, only the fear of reprisal and some occasional public nod to ethics really keep order in international affairs. Mere promises have no value beyond the moment, only the deed. Remember that.

In the narrow seas, any extra-regional naval force which appears is most apt to be an open ocean, blue water one, made up of larger ships and craft. It will be projecting power across distance, under- and mis-armed for many of its tasks. Meeting some or all of these tasks may on the other hand be best done by local allies, with or without big power assistance.

In the narrow seas, any intra-regional force is apt to be made up of smaller ships and craft, controlling only coastal white and brown riverine waters, if any. This is true even of local fractions of larger navies. But the best of them will be tailored for their task.

INSHORE OPERATIONS

All waters within the narrow seas tend to take on the fundamental characteristics of inshore waters. Operations in these waters involve large numbers of the smaller naval ships and craft to a degree initially not always realized by Mahanian (big ship, blue water) navies.

Along the narrow seas, once sovereignty (law and order) has been established, it has almost certainly to be defended, other state interests have to be secured, and other policy supported by a navy. Although now emphasizing somewhat higher-intensity war-fighting duties, the navy's internal security and public service functions remain with it.

In near waters like these, fleets have six main wartime tasks:

- patrol of river and coastal waters;
- escort of coastal convoys;
- minelaying, offensive as well as defensive;
- minesweeping, clearing one's own as well as enemy mines, keeping the necessary sea-lanes open;
- support of land operations (small amphibious efforts, raids, naval gunfire support), acting as the seaward flank of the army; and
- logistic support of other military forces.

In the most grandiose terms, this becomes sea control/sea denial and power projection. These are mini-versions, sometimes hardly recognizable as such. Projection is really strike. Yes. But for small navies, this is a big job.

All of these six inshore tasks assume for their success some measure of a perhaps rudimentary but well practised AA and ASW capability. All are best carried out under the protection of a closely cooperating naval air arm.

Meeting any one or even two of these assumptions may be well beyond a particular small navy, but most do better and all are capable of unpleasant surprises.

SMALL NAVIES, PER SE

What might a small narrow seas navy look like? The multiplication of submarine warfare capabilities among an expanding list of Third World navies signifies that the most complex form of war at sea—ASW—has become even more complex. Submarines, purposes, and owners have all proliferated. Moreover, these small navies still have to satisfy requirements other than ASW. There will accordingly be much continued interest in multi-role platforms and weapon systems.

FACs can be small, cheap, seaworthy, fast, carry a variety of weapons, and pack a heavy punch—but they cannot really maximize all six things at once. Optimum designs depend heavily upon the specific geographic and military environment(s) in which the boats are to operate, the roles they will have to perform, and the budget available. For every small navy, hard choices will have had to be made, each time.

Sea-based/sea-related air support will be another crucial problem. This one will remain with a force throughout its existence. Cooperation with aircraft from an independent air force—the most usual situation—is notoriously chancy, at best. It will need to be carefully prepared beforehand, and frequently practiced. An organic air arm will be much sought after.

Small diesel electric submarines are desirable defensive weapons for any navy. They are, however, expensive, high tech weapons, beyond the procurement budget or maintenance capability of most small navies. They will nonetheless be much sought after.

A coherent, agreed strategy for these smaller navies is both a procurement and an operational necessity. Platforms and weapons to do what? The more steps there are in the naval escalation ladder (the more choices they have) the more maneuverability national decision makers have.

Missiles—like torpedoes—are all-or-nothing weapons. Ton for ton, even a diesel submarine is the most expensive warship money can buy. Leaders need to decide what the most appropriate mix of high tech missiles and basic guns might be. Can tasks assigned to submarines not be covered some other way?

The policing of newly acquired frontier zones calls for a good reach, but the punch can be light. Mere presence and the ability to put a shot across the bow is usually more important than the ability to cripple or sink.

Limited sea denial operations directed against a hostile regional or even local power may involve nothing more than sporadic hit-and-run tactics, and mining, ensuring that the enemy does not enjoy full control of the sea.

There is always a caveat, however. Lesser navies need to be particularly careful in that scenario-driven plans—of necessity cut to the bone—tend somehow not ever to cover whatever really does arise. Hardware choices must insofar as possible allow for this.

Dominant regional powers have a particularly difficult strategic problem—having to look not one but two ways. They must always be able to take on local navies with forces appropriate to the various challenges. They must also, however, be able to face intervention by extraregional blue water navies. Both can mean wherever possible holding the gates to their sea. Otherwise, the requirements of these two divergent missions may not be the same.

THE U.S. PROBLEM

The Soviet–U.S. cold war went into formal remission in 1988. Arms are being reduced, on all sides, as "peace dividends" are being reallocated. We have in any case long been moving from a highly politicized and threatening bipolar world to one that is becoming much less stable, even more politicized, albeit one with a much more relaxed East-West attitude. The world is still threatening, but in a different way, in new areas.

The United States is therefore today restructuring its military's power projection, expeditionary, and mobility forces. In direct question are the navy's aircraft carrier battle groups, the marine corps, and the army's airborne and light infantry divisions. One way or another, they will be affected the most.

Behind this remains the residual Russian threat. We still face long-term competition with the Soviets. There are many areas where fundamental Russian interests do not entirely coincide with those of the United States. This will always be the case. U.S. interest and reach will continue to have to be demonstrated from time to time.

A cornerstone of NATO general war strategy has been to establish early sea control in the Norwegian Sea, as far forward as possible. This would be primarily a U.S. effort. NATO would thereby protect the North Atlantic sea-lanes, block the deployment of the Soviet Navy from its northern bases, and back up Allied land forces on Europe's northern flank.[1]

Although the threat is today somewhat more remote, the strategy remains a sound one. As the United States draws down our forces in Europe, the ability to rebuild these forces over there becomes more critical. With more mobilization lead time, much of the full-time active army, and some of the air force can be drafted to the reserve. Even some of the navy's surface fleet and ASW air can be shifted to the reserve, but they certainly cannot entirely be given up. Sea- and airlift increase in importance. NATO must maintain an adequate European base infrastructure, ready to receive us back on little notice.

We cannot abandon the forward strategy and pull back to a more relaxed policy of ASW patrols in the Greenland-Iceland-UK gap, as some have suggested. There would be no surer way for NATO to lose both Iceland and Norway.

But we now need to shift the immediate emphasis of our strategy. We no longer need to field large land and air forces on short notice in Europe. As non-NATO contingencies become more likely, we need more quick response forces, worldwide. For this there can be only one viable option: the maritime option, built around our navy.

THE MARITIME OPTION

The U.S. Navy—like all navies—has in the most general terms four functions: presence, sea control/sea denial, power projection, and deterrence. It is now necessary for the U.S. to reassess what it is we still need to defend with the threat of violence, or with violence itself. Then we will have to decide how we will do it, employing which of the shrinking arsenal of tools still available to us. We then have to cut back to a balanced force that can satisfy these needs.

Balanced force reductions do not of themselves mean *equal* cuts for all services. Rationally, since we are talking overseas commitments, the navy, marines, and air force (and coast guard for its own reasons) should face the smallest cuts, if any. In any case, resources will have to be shifted.

The United States will for the forseeable future have to rely on the maritime option for most of its forward projection and expeditionary forces. As Americans with an eye to our own navy, it is this latter scenario which must concern us most here. For our merchantmen as well as for our naval vessels, what is the actual maritime threat? How can we best handle it?

It is possible to sketch the rough outline of our naval requirements now and through at least the next decade. A prudent portion (one-half?) of our strength will have to remain ready to fight high-intensity blue water war, to keep the art alive, to face the worst possible case, and to give cover to the rest. One-quarter will have to be made up of low-intensity conflict-specialized forces. The remaining quarter can be general purpose forces.

Such a breakdown provides for the most likely case—low-intensity limited and sub-limited war in narrow seas. It calls for conventional forces—not nuclear. There is a premium on numbers. But numbers of what?

UNFAMILIAR WATERS

Today the most pressing single task the United States faces is to develop a narrow seas strategy and the tools to carry it out. The collective and long-term effects of low-intensity naval conflict—as expressed in insurgencies, counterinsurgencies, terrorism, and low-level regional hostilities—represent a genuine danger to our interests. Countless low-intensity conflicts smolder and flare around the world, and they will continue to do so. They will have to be dealt with.

In the coming multi-polar world—much less dominated by superpower competition, much more disturbed by old and new local grievances—the United States will face a variety of naval challenges from increasingly well armed smaller powers. The United States thus needs to be prepared to face a whole spectrum of highly politicized low-intensity conflict. This will include brushfire wars and restricted regional troubles. The boundaries of this politico-military spectrum can easily be set, along with requirements for an adequate response:

- quick responses with small specialized forces to sudden crises like terrorist hijackings, on the one hand; and
- somewhat more deliberate responses with conventional force to more complex situations, on the other.

Achille Lauro represents the bottom end of this spectrum, while the Persian Gulf can be taken to stand for the top.

Along this spectrum we will face self-designated popular fronts as well as established states.

Outright U.S. intervention can be quick-hitting, blunt, massive, and brief (Grenada in 1983). It can also be gradual, low-key, slow, and long-term (the Persian Gulf 1987–88). Most intervention will take place in and along the narrow seas. Basically, to the United States these are unfamiliar waters. That will have to change.

Strategic preoccupation with super-war, and overintensive specialization, has led to a steady erosion of that inherent flexibility which is one of the prime characteristics of properly developed seapower. Either the navy's responsibilities or its future plans should be brought into line before we suffer worse embarrassments than those in the Persian Gulf. Nor just our interests, but our reputation is at stake.

Neither *Bridgeton* nor *Roberts* need have been mined. Neither *Stark* nor *Vincennes* had air cover.

We need also to develop close contacts with the smaller navies, ensuring a safe base from which to operate within those narrow seas, and their cooperation in there, filling out our probably permanent need for additional ships and craft at the lower end.

A temporarily diverted Marine helicopter assault ship (39,000 tons) was simply too large for the constricted maneuvering area available to her in the Gulf (see Appendix B). Her air group being ad hoc also lessened its value. She was just all we could provide for inside.

Whatever we do, we will have to avoid repeating the spectacle of again having a merchantman we were supposedly escorting (*Bridgeton*)—already mined while in our care—lead our combatants to safety while the whole world looked on.

Our capabilities for this kind of operation will need to be able from now on to stand on their own. We cannot any longer always depend on support from our allies. The warning flags are up.

THE SHAPE OF SHIPS TO COME

Face it. Any big power—not just the United States—that might actually be embroiled in these waters will have to provide a force that looks much the same as the small navy it faces. We are all operating under what often turn out to be quite similar internal and external political and economic curbs. Perhaps more directly relevant, militarily, too, there are very similar constraints, geographically and tactically. Working to keep a supernavy's capital ships on a short line in these narrow seas, low-intensity wars is a convergence of factors, all of which add up to the same thing:

- the generally unstable international environment, described earlier;
- the specific issues ordinarily at stake (important, yes, but seldom vital);
- the specific enemy (small) and the forces (limited) at his disposal;
- the high cost of capital ship replacement in a time of universally severe budget constraints;
- the sheer time (up to ten years) required to replace major losses, if replaced they ever are; and
- the ready availability of cheaper, more expendable substitute types.

No extra-regional power—especially one having an essentially open ocean, blue water big-ship navy—will either want or be able to commit its entire fleet to such a war. It will continue to have assorted interests elsewhere which will still require at least a presence. There may even be other active threats, some more serious than the one in hand.

Super-threats demand super-carriers. Lesser threats can be met adequately with light (probably V/STOL) carriers. In the narrow seas, they can often be better—or even only—met with these smaller flat tops. Three of these carriers together with their escorts could cost no more than one super-carrier task group, by the by.

THE RECORD

The idea of using light carriers in narrow seas conflict almost always signals the opening of loud and hot debate. Wardrooms split. Enemies are made. The gruff old big-ship salts simply brush the idea aside as a myth. But look at the record. There can be little real question. Yes, U.S. and Japanese capital ships were committed to face each other in the close confines of the Coral Sea and the Solomons (both in 1942). The same was true again at Leyte (1944). Yes, there have been U.S. super-carriers in the Mediterranean since the late 1940s. Yes, we plan to send four super-carriers into the Norwegian Sea in a general war.

But in WWII, the issues were vital ones, nothing less than survival of the two ways of life; in the Coral Sea and the Solomons and again at Leyte, the risk had to be taken. As far as the Sixth Fleet's carriers today go, their role is primarily a political one; in any major war, they would have either to pull out or be written off. In the meantime, for a narrow sea the Mediterranean is a relatively big place; there is some room for maneuver. Otherwise, if we ever did send carriers into the Norwegian Sea, in a general war, it would take at least four to stay there.

Still looking at the record, has the United States committed either a super-carrier or even a battleship to inside the Persian Gulf, for any reason, in any of our recent crises? Despite the mass of naval power assembled outside Hormuz, not even the seizure of our Teheran embassy and the holding hostage of fifty-two of its staff for 444 days (1979–80) or our abortive attempt to rescue them (1980) could get us to send the really big boys in.

No super-carrier has ever been inside the gulf. In December 1989, battleship *New Jersey* finally entered the gulf on a routine flag-showing operation, to demonstrate a continuing U.S. commitment to the region. This was the first time such a U.S. warship had sailed the sensitive waterway in modern times. That speaks for itself. The record is clear, for those who will see.

OPERATIONS

The hazards of exposure to the wide arsenal of lethal weaponry available today and in the hands of a frightening number of small navies, coupled with the timeless threat posed by navigation in shallow, cramped, badly marked narrow seas will continue, if not grow.

Any superpower contemplating combat operations in these waters—force projection and/or just sea control—will face the same dilemma. Unless one can come in overwhelming force, and there is sufficient maneuver room deep water to bring it to bear; unless one is willing to risk possibly crushing losses, considering the possible gains; an outsider has little choice. Survival of our way of life will seldom again be the issue, in our time. Bets will have to be hedged, losses kept down.

Any big power force steaming here into harm's way will, therefore, have to be tailored to the task. While as upscale as it dares and can manage to be, it will have to look in the end a lot like the indigenous navy it faces. There will have to be FACs, minesweepers, and as much landbased air as it can scrape up and base. To this might be added V/STOL carriers, destroyers, frigates, a minelayer, an amphibious unit, even a cruiser or submarine.

In operating out there, we ourselves need always to exploit the geography of the narrow seas. Insofar as possible, we need to keep out of these seas, operating instead off the entrances with our deep sea ships. We need to exploit our built-in capability for blockade, at those entrances.

We need to continue to exploit our superior air power, declining to operate without continuous CAP, inside or out. We need to develop a better shallow water ASW capability/torpedo defense. For this we need a considerably expanded V/STOL capability, to include small carriers. We need a truly independent mine warfare capability. We need a better area surveillance capability. And we need to learn to think in small war politico-military terms. This is, after all, not simply *naval* but complex *maritime* war we are talking about.

We need also to make every effort to encourage those small

countries to organize navies suited to best meeting their own real needs as well as to complement our own. This usally means coast guards, at first, and only after that lean, mean war-fighting fleets. Such an approach coincides with the best interests of both. Basic internal security puts down insurgencies, and thereby provides pirates with both less opportunity and less legitimation for terrorism at sea. Too few have such a navy.

If the future U.S. fleet we have described resembles the Zumwalt high-low ship mix first proposed in the 1970s, that is no accident.[2] The concept may have been premature then, but it appears to fit the situation now.

As the use of military force comes ever more to involve political constraints, swift, well executed intervention from the sea—raids, sea-based counterinsurgency, rescues, surgical strikes, visits—can provide a discriminating use of force, and high gain at little cost. The navy's role will if anything grow.

No matter what is done, any U.S. intervention will have to begin, be accompanied by, and finish with continuous battle area surveillance, making battle area management possible. This will involve the probable necessity to land base airborne warning and control planes somewhere within range.

FINISHED WITH ENGINES

We in the United States need to be aware. The combination of mines with aircraft is similar in importance to the joining of torpedo with submarine or missile with ship. All three of these natural combinations of weaponry with platform occurred within only the last one hundred years. Their implications have not yet been fully integrated with the main body of naval strategy.

So we have in this book dealt with the narrow seas, small navies, and fat merchantmen. This essay cannot be the end, only a start, for dealing with these issues. It aims to open up thought, not close it.

In the world as it is and will be—not as we would wish it to be—the narrow seas will continue to be most dangerous places. We superpowers will visit there, to deliver or to pick up. We will fish and on occasion explore. Our merchantmen will pass through there, en route somewhere else, on our lawful occasions in other far places. We will support allies, and discourage our enemies.

Under these conditions, the best guarantee of safety for all concerned will lie in our knowing and understanding these seas, these small navies, as a start.

Then we will need to be ready with the right kinds of seapower to defend successfully our legitimate interests there, under those special conditions we will certainly face. Not only the right kinds, but enough of them.

In these waters, all operations require continuous, adequate air cover. We are not exempt.

In these waters, all operations require minesweeping escort. We are not exempt.

Bridgeton, *Stark*, and *Roberts* were unnecessary losses. I would like to think that this book could help better prepare for next time.

NOTES

1. John F. Lehman, Jr., *Command of the Seas* (New York: Charles Scribner's Sons, 1988), pp. 115–45.

2. Elmo R. Zumwalt, Jr., *On Watch* (New York: Quadrangle/The New York Times Book Co., 1976), pp. 72–84.

Appendix A

Inshore Waters and Narrow Seas

THE NARROW SEAS

The waters off every coast which are significantly affected by the land as well as the sea form a special theater of war—the inshore area. In the narrow seas, these waters extend from one shore across to the other, giving the whole body the characteristics of inshore waters. Here, unlike on the high seas, there is close and continuous interaction between events ashore and at sea.

The geographic extent of such theaters cannot be rigidly defined. Nonetheless, in most cases today they reach out some 300 to 500 miles. Their specific extent depends in each case on the power and operational range of all the lighter, cheaper weapons of naval warfare present; mining and sweeping capabilities of those involved; the range and capabilities of committed aircraft, especially shore-based planes.

On these waters—offshore and inshore, both loosely called "inshore"—is fought the white water (offshore) and brown water (river and estuarine) naval war. This is a unique kind of war. Land-based air power—today including shore-based missiles—plays a major role, in both strategy and tactics. But mastery here sooner or later is a *sine qua non* to exploitation of seapower.

In case anyone forgets, sea lines of communication—also otherwise known militarily by the horrible acronym SLOCs—is really what this or any other book about navies is in the end all about. Despite the tremendous number of people now moved by air, despite the great boom in high-value/low-bulk air cargo, almost all the world's food, fibers, minerals, manufactures, and fuel is still moved by sea on ships. These ships tend to travel known routes, running from, to, and between established ports. These routes make up the lines of communication—the sea-lanes.

As the valuable and defenseless merchantmen plod along the SLOCs, they are sooner or later bound to travel one or more of the narrow seas. There they are dependent for their safety first on the generally small navies of the littoral states. Only if diplomatic recourse fails will the Great Powers intervene here.

As a matter of fact, any outside intervention, for whatever political, military, economic, or trade reason, will depend for 95 percent of its food, ammunition, fuel, and other supplies on the sea. These, too, will sooner or later cross one or more of the narrow seas. There the way will be cleared for them—the mines swept, the submarines and planes driven off—by those same lesser navies.

The narrow seas particularly provide cheap, convenient water routes to, from, and between points on their rim. These same seas provide routes for transient shipping through the land masses they divide. They are fishing grounds. They are sites for oil and gas drilling, and mining. Violence is endemic.

Few U.S. naval thinkers since Mahan have paid much attention to the narrow seas, and Mahan was interested mainly in the Panama Canal and waters to our immediate south. This, despite our experience in the Seminole Indian Wars (1832–42), the War Between the States (1861–65), and all the wars since.

Nonetheless, the land portions of the world are belted by a ring of such seas, roughly dividing north from south. Not all of these are in fact called seas, some are designated as gulfs; some are more properly oceans; but they all share the same essential characteristics: the Gulf of Mexico and the Caribbean; the Mediterranean (including the Adriatic and Aegean) and Black Seas; the Red Sea and its dependent Gulf of Aqaba; the Straits of Malacca; the Java, Banda, Timor, and Arafura Seas; the Bismarck and Coral Seas, to name the most important of them.

Other narrow seas provide major "re-entrants" (in real military terms) into Europe, the Middle and Far East: the English Channel and the North Sea, the Danish Straits (Skagerrak and Kattegat), the Baltic with the Gulfs of Bothnia, Finland and Riga, and Danzig Bay; the Adriatic, Aegian and Black Seas; the Persian Gulf; the Gulf of Siam; the South and East China Seas and the Po Hai; the Sea of Japan; and the Sea of Okhotsk.

The icebound North Polar seas share many of the more important characteristics of narrow seas and are of great potential strategic value. Leading into them are three major sea routes. Along Eurasia's western rim lie the Greenland and Norwegian Seas. Along its eastern rim lie the Bering Sea, Bering Strait, and Chukchi Sea. These also border North America's western shore. Along North America's eastern shore lie the Labrador Sea, Davis Strait, and Baffin Bay. These are themselves narrow seas.

As already mentioned, these narrow seas all share one characteristic: unlike the deep oceans, they are all important fishing grounds. Fishermen are everywhere, looking for scallops, cod, sardines; or yellow-tail, shrimp, what have you.

For our purposes, narrow seas can be divided now militarily into three general groups. The first includes those dominated by a single navy superpower, like the Sea of Okhotsk and the Po Hai. So, sometimes does the Black Sea. These inevitably take on the aspects of a closed sea.

The second group takes in those dominated by no one power, but which are bordered by a variety of lesser states exercising more or less control over their contiguous waters. These seas carry the widest possible variety of international maritime traffic. Witness the Mediterranean, the Red Sea, and the Persian Gulf, among others. Included here are strategic international straits such as Dover, the Skagerrak/Kattegat, Gibraltar, Otranto, the Bosphorous/Dardanelles, Tiran, el-Mandeb, Hormuz, and Malacca; canals such as Panama and Suez, and the like.

The last group encompasses those seas which count a littoral superpower but which share the sea with other, lesser states. These waters are vital to all these states—the Black and Baltic Seas, the Caribbean, and the China Seas. These take on a mixture of the characteristics exhibited by both previous groups of seas.

On the Mahanian high seas, blue water naval strategy and tactics are effectively played out on a gameboard with no significant geographic or hydrographic features other than limitless water and a bottom stretching almost to infinity (12,000 feet?). Manuever is operationally unconstrained, except for such rudimentary rules as be up sun and down moon, and hold the weather gauge. The land plays no direct role in whatever takes place. There are as a rule no neutrals or civilian bystanders to worry about. Most large navies think of themselves as blue water forces, defining their roles in Mahanian terms. This is *naval* war.

On the narrow seas, this "pure" naval strategy is modified in a number of fundamental ways:

- entrance to and exits from these seas can be controlled, usually from the land;
- land-based aircraft and missiles become major factors in sea-oriented operations;
- land-based radar becomes important;
- mines become a major factor;
- maneuver is constrained, especially for deep-draft ships;
- there is little room for large ships to run and no place for them to hide;
- smaller ships and craft (specifically including light carriers, fast attack craft, small diesel submarines, and landing craft) become important major players, for the first time; and
- operations are much more politicized.

All this (and more) stems from the fact that in narrow seas the land itself plays a major role, interacting continually and directly with the sea. Distances in these waters are generally shorter, the water is as a rule shallower (there *is* a bottom), and the seas are usually calmer. There are sand bars, rocks, reefs, headlands, islands, ports and harbors, canals and rivers, and people. Blue water rules can apply, but only in a bastardized fashion, and new ones add on. This is *maritime* war.

Thus, here, the playboard is not just a flat featureless expanse of water. The character of these waters is intricate, governed by the nature of the coast, the nature and location of the natural traffic choke points (straits), the number and location of the harbors, and the depths. The weather and the sea itself play a big part.

Submarines do not like to operate in the shallow waters characteristic of narrow seas. But in the narrow seas, anti-submarine warfare (ASW) poses its own special problems. These waters are marked by high ambient noise, turbulent currents, fresh water runoff, sometimes high turbidity, very confused salinity layers, and old wrecks. The shallow bottom is a two-edged sword.

Most big ship navies employ weapons and sensors oriented toward blue water ASW. There the water is always over 600 feet deep, and often over 6000 feet.

Powerful hull-mounted deep water low-frequency sonars achieve ranges sometimes measured in hundreds of miles through open ocean. But in shallow coastal areas, these same sonars are often blind, their sonar signals tending to bounce right back off the seabed, blanking out the sonar operator's screen. Air-dropped variable depth sonobuoys often work better under these conditions. So do helicopter-borne high frequency dipping sonars.

That is not all. ASW torpedoes—along with depth charges, the major ASW weapons—themselves sometimes do not function well in shallow water. All too often their active homing sonar reportedly guides the torpedo in on the seabed returns rather than on those from any submarine target.

Here the coast is flat and featureless also, or it is not. There are islands, and/or sand banks, mud flats, rock pinnacles, leads, shoals, reefs. There are headlands, natural traffic choke points behind which lurk who knows what. There are straits, natural funnels through which all shipping must pass. The main shipping lanes are clearly marked and well-known. They pass close to shore or they do not. Ports and harbors are many or few. They are icebound or killing hot. Deep water encourages submarine operation, shallow water—really shallow—mining. There are currents and tides. Too strong for mining? No problem? To the always sufficient natural hazards to navigation, in time of war must be added those contributed by man. Air power will be a factor. Whose? Submarines will be a factor. Whose? In both cases, where and how? Ports can be covered by hostile artillery, or missiles, or not.

These narrow seas all share one common feature—they all have limited access, usually through one or more maritime choke points: Gibraltar, Suez, el-Mandeb, Singapore, Panama, Yucatan, Florida, or the like. The Kiel and Corinth Canals give additional access, the one to the Baltic and the other to the Ionian Sea. The Sicilian Channel and the Strait of Messina divide the Mediterranean in two. Control of these access points gives any military power substantial control of the sea beyond.

Appendix B

Navigation in the Persian Gulf

At sea, adding always to the dangers created by man are the more fundamental and timeless ones of nature. A final word must, therefore, be said about the Persian Gulf area itself. The gulf's harsh environment—searing summer heat, high water temperatures, dust clouds, sudden and violent winter storms, and always the sand—inevitably adds to the difficulty of accomplishing any task out there.

The Persian Gulf is an arm of the Arabian Sea running generally northwest-southeast, lying between Iran, to the north, and Arabia, to the south. Some 500 miles long, it varies from fifty to 200 miles in width, with an average depth of only one hundred feet. It is shallower at the upper and than the lower. It is connected at the lower end with the Gulf of Oman by the Strait of Hormuz; Iran lies on one side there and the Sultanate of Oman on the other. The strait is only less than thirty miles in width but has an even narrower deep-draft channel.

As we have said, the gulf is shallow. Within the gulf, depth rarely exceeds forty or fifty fathoms; it decreases to thirty and twenty fathoms towards the head. For one-third of the gulf, especially off the Arabian coast, depth is less than twenty fathoms, with many and very irregular soundings, shallow banks, and shoals. There are hundreds of small islands scattered about. Deep draft routes are few, and well known.

Today, with shallow waters on the Arabian side and an exclusion zone declared by Iran on the other, large ships such as tankers in effect are restricted to a narrow fairway down the gulf's center.

In ballast, however, between Bahrain and Kuwait, large ships *can* thread their way close along the Arabian coast, although this is time-consuming, difficult, even dangerous. The second upbound U.S. convoy apparently did just that, to avoid the Farsi area (1987).

Out here, winters tend to be mild and short, and the summers long and hot, very hot. What little rain there is comes in winter. In summer the skies are almost permanently clear. Fog is rare, but dust haze is frequent. The water tends to be very clear; underwater hazards can be easily seen. The sea gets up quickly, and is short, with sometimes strong swells.

Winds from between west and north predominate throughout the year, light to moderate. Strong winds (force 6 and over) occur, but are largely confined to the first six months of the year; this is the Shamal, sometimes creating short storms.

Most of the time, current through the Strait of Hormuz flows opposite, westerly into the gulf. Tidal streams reach four knots at the strait, with eddies and races, less elsewhere.

Current flows westerly along the northern shore of the gulf, too. Generally the rate does not exceed one knot, but occasional stronger currents may be met. The probable maximum is about 1.5 knots.

Everywhere the water is warm; more so, of course, in summer than winter. Most of the water input comes from the Tigris and Euphrates Rivers, by way of the Shall-al-Arab, in the extreme northwest. No great amount exits, due to evaporation; what does, goes out through the Strait of Hormuz as highly saline bottom water.

Commercial shipping here follows a surprisingly regular pattern. Imports from the outside world (manufactures, food, fibers) travel along the waterway's main axis, as does the outgoing oil and gas which pays for them, in large modern ships. Local traffic—still moving in ancient dhows, as a rule—tends to travel across the main axis. Everyone fishes, everywhere.

Throughout the gulf there are numerous oil and gas rigs, both drilling and production platforms, as could be expected. Most of them exhibit lights and sound fog signals. These are shown on large-scale charts, and often their flares are visible for miles. There are others, however, that are uncharted and unlit.

Electronic navigation possibilities are good, however. Decca (a British commercial hyperbolic radio positioning system) reaches the length of the gulf, even covering the gulf entrance. The strait also boasts a

VTS, complete with traffic separation and radar surveillance, under Omani control.

Most aids to navigation here are positioned and kept up by a gulf-wide commercial company—Middle East Navigation Aids Service. Increasingly, however, aids are being taken over by national authorities. There is a commerical gulf pilot service based out of Khor Fakkan. Notwithstanding the many modern improvements, operations here are a continual strain, even the simplest ones.

Appendix C

V-22 Makes Small Carriers Viable

Navies—small or large—require aircraft carriers—small or large—for two basic reasons: air defense and strike. Air defense means a combat air patrol (CAP) with the task group or force., As we know, even a shore-based fighter on strip alert only 200 miles away would need 20 minutes to reach combat altitude over ships under attack. There can also be little projection of force without a capability for strike.

The smaller powers operate *small* (12,000–22,000-ton) aircraft carriers, if any. That is the best they can afford. The larger powers require *small* carriers as well as big ones because in certain situations they dare not risk their effectively irreplaceable big (90,000–100,000-ton) carriers, or there is just not enough depth of water or sea room for the big carriers to work.

Small carriers can operate a nominal air group of up to twenty aircraft, basically in some mix of fighter-bombers and/or ASW helicopters. In a few cases—notably in the Royal Navy—a small number of helos have been converted to the AEW role, but this is not the rule. Most small carriers—of necessity—operate in the STOVL mode, flying VSTOL aircraft.

Small carriers—conventional or VSTOL—tend to be simple floating garages. They lack catapults, for instance. But the VSTOL carriers have a forward "ski-jump" ramp that allows STOVL operations, doubling the allowable ordnance-fuel take-off weight.

Carriers smaller than, say, 12,000 tons can be built and operated, but under these conditions deck space becomes a limiting factor. Continuous flight operations for them become effectively out of the question.

Small carriers thus have a serious inbred problem—they *are* small. On the open ocean when employed in the convoy escort–ASW role, their size does not seem to matter much. For this they are large enough to carry sufficient helos, and even a few subsonic *Harriers* to chase off the lone, shadowing, over-the-horizon, long-range, maritime patrol aircraft or bomber.

Closer to shore—especially when used in the power projection role—the size of small carriers becomes a more serious matter. For this, they are just not powerful enough for the task. This limits their general utility.

It is no secret that the world is being stuffed with land-based, high-performance fighter-bombers. Even the smallest countries can be counted on to have at least a few. These fighter-bombers will often be armed with, among other things, air-to-surface antiship missiles. Small carriers are vulnerable even to just a medium-sized conventional "iron" bomb or two, never mind antiship missiles.

In this role, a single small carrier group in the narrow seas can operate only at great risk, even if the on-board aircraft mix is weighted heavily toward fighters. There would probably just never be enough of them to operate a sufficient continuous overhead combat air patrol, or to absorb the inevitable operational losses. Two carriers are much (three times?) better, one to carry out the CAP and ASW missions, the other to fly the strike tasks. Three are even better, but even then, probably not enough.

Three of these small carriers together with the necessary surface escorts could cost as much as a single supercarrier with its escorts. Three small carrier air groups add up to some sixty aircraft; a large carrier's air wing runs about eighty. The small carrier's planes generally must be VSTOL; the large carrier's planes are high performance. This alone explains some of the reluctance of the Western powers to build small carriers, especially when the present surface control environment and resulting combat efficiency of the small group is considered. What to do?

The Royal Navy managed to sail a small (two-carrier) task force against the Argentines in 1982, and barely managed to win back the Falklands (Malvinas). If the Argentines with their *Mirages* had struck first for air superiority rather than boring straight in for the transports, the result would probably have been different.

Having had the need for some sort of force multiplier now made very apparent to them, the British rushed conversion of a small number of *Sea King* helos into AEW copters, notably mounting a *Searchwater* air-to-air and air-to-surface radar. But a helo is the wrong platform for AEW: Maximum altitude is too low; endurance is too short; vibration is too great; and the cabin is too small and too noisy for the admittedly cheaper helo to do a really good job. In any case, the AEW *Sea Kings* were too late for the Falklands campaign.

A proper naval airborne warning and control system (AWACS) accompanies the fleet. It multiplies the effectiveness of a given number of fighters by many times. It can automatically track several hundred targets against any background, land or sea. It can mon˙tor ships at sea down to patrol boat in size. It earns its deck space.

A naval AWACS extends the radar horizon by lifting the control radar from the surface up to 25,000 feet, thus from 50 to around 250 miles, giving from 10 to 30 minutes more air warning time. This allows fighters to be kept on deck alert, not always in the air. The AWACS alone need fly continuous (or near continuous) cover over a force. It gives the force sufficient opportunity to upgrade its defense to maximum readiness.

Large flat-deck carriers have settled the AWACS problem. U.S. carriers carry the fixed-wing conventional turbo-prop-driven E-2C *Hawkeye*, a medium-sized plane smaller than the Air Force's large E-3 *Sentry*, but with the capabilities of the naval AWACS described above—adequate for the job.

The AWACS issue has been settled by the land-based air forces. In the Persian Gulf, against Iran, Saudi Arabia's land-based E-3s were invaluable, helping surveil both surface and air, extending the radar horizon to 600 miles.

Israel flies E-2Cs. So does Egypt. And they have no airfield space problem: Against Syria, Israel's E-2Cs have proven well their worth. But you cannot fly even E-2Cs off small carriers. It is too much plane.

The new Bell-Boeing V-22 *Osprey* VSTOL (turbo-prop tilt-rotor) is the VSTOL answer to an on-board AEW plane for small carriers. The *Osprey* can provide performance comparable to that of the E-2C. The V-22's twin engines allow it to cruise at 275 knots, with a nominal range of 500 miles. The V-22 weighs only 32,000 pounds in its basic (truck) configuration; to this must be added a 7,000-pound AEW radar. It can fly with a gross weight of 55,000 pounds. The phased array antennas are mounted outside on both sides, just behind the wing.

The V-22 *Osprey* is a revolutionary new aircraft. This aircraft flies twice as fast as a helo, twice as far, more than twice as high, and requires half the maintenance. It is large and relatively roomy, and

Selected Bibliography

Abel, Elie. *The Missile Crisis*. Philadelphia: J. B. Lippincott, 1966. The Cuban missiles.

Ackley, Richard T. "Remembering the Diesel." *U.S. Naval Institute Proceedings* (July 1989). 96–100. Diesel submarines.

Agar, Augustus. *Baltic Episode*. London: Conway Maritime Press, 1983. Coastal motor boats 1919–20.

Bally, Jacques J. "Understanding the Independent NATO Partner." *U.S. Naval Institute Proceedings* (June 1989): 72–78. The French Navy and NATO.

Beaufre, André. *Strategy of Action*. Translated by R. H. Barry. London: Faber and Faber, 1966.

Bennett, Geoffrey. *Cowan's War*. London: Collins, 1964. The Royal Navy in the Baltic 1919–20.

Bragadin, Marc'Antonio. *The Italian Navy in World War II*. Annapolis, MD: U.S. Naval Institute, 1957.

Breyer, Siegfried and Peter Joachim Lapp. *Die Volksmarine der DDR*. Koblenz: Bernard & Graefe, 1985. Growth from maritime police to navy.

Brodie, Bernard. *A Guide to Naval Strategy*. 5th ed. New York: Praeger, 1965.

Brooks, Ewart. *Prologue to a War*. London: White Lion, 1977. Norway 1940.

Buckley, Robert J., Jr. *At Close Quarters*. Washington: Naval History Division, 1962. PT boats.

Cable, James. "The Freedom of the Baltic." *Navy International* (May 1989): 225–27.

Carver, Michael. *War Since 1945*. New York: G. P. Putnam's Sons, 1981.

Cocchia, Aldo. *The Hunters and the Hunted*. Annapolis, MD: U.S. Naval Institute, 1958. Italy's *Regia Marina* in WWII.

Corbett, Julian S. *Some Principles of Maritime Strategy*. Annapolis, MD: Naval Institute Press, 1972.

Corbett, Percy Elwood. *The Study of International Law*. Short Studies in Political Science. Garden City, NY: Doubleday, 1955.

Cutler, Thomas J. *Brown Water, Black Berets*. Annapolis, MD: Naval Institute Press, 1988. U.S. riverine Vietnam.

Defense Mapping Agency H/TC. *Red Sea and Persian Gulf*. SD Pub. 172; Washington: Government Printing Office, 1986.

Elliott, Peter. *Allied Minesweeping in World War 2*. Annapolis, MD: Naval Institute Press, 1979.

Fock, Harald. *Fast Fighting Boats 1870–1945*. Annapolis, MD: Naval Institute Press, 1978.

Gretton, Peter. *Maritime Strategy*. New York: Praeger, 1965.

Griffiths, Maurice. *The Hidden Menace*. Greenwich, England: Conway Maritime Press, 1981. Mines past, present, and future.

Hartmann, Gregory K. *Weapons That Wait*. Annapolis, MD: Naval Institute Press, 1979. Mines in the U.S. Navy.

Heyl, Phillip J. "Costa Rica's Emerging Coast Guard." *U.S. Naval Institute Proceedings* (April 1989): 113–16.

Hezlet, Arthur. *Aircraft and Sea Power*. New York: Stein and Day, 1970.

Hill, J. R. *Maritime Strategy for Medium Powers*. Annapolis, MD: Naval Institute Press, 1986.

Irving, David. *The Destruction of Convoy PQ.17*. New York: Simon and Schuster, 1968. The costliest Murmansk run.

Jackson, Robert. *Suez 1956: Operation Musketeer*. London: Ian Allan, 1980.

Johnson, Ellis A. and David A. Katcher. *Mines Against Japan*. White Oak, MD: Naval Ordnance Laboratory, 1973.

Keegan, John. *The Price of Admiralty*. New York: Viking, 1988.

Koburger, Charles W., Jr. "Morning Coats and Brass Hats." *Military Review* (April 1965): 65–74.

———. *Sea Power in the Falklands*. New York: Praeger, 1983. The 1982 war at sea.

———. *Steel Hulls, Iron Crosses, and Refugees*. New York: Praeger, 1989. Germany's *Kriegsmarine* in the Baltic 1939–45.

———. "Swords and Surfboats." *Proceedings*. Maritime Law Enforcement Seminar held in London in November 1983.

Leggett, Eric. *The Corfu Incident*. London: PBS, 1974.

Lehman, John R., Jr. *Command of the Sea*. New York: Charles Scribner's Sons, 1988.

Le Masne de Chermont (Captain). "Les Frégates de Surveillance." *Cols Blues* (April–May 1989): 14–16.

Lenton, H. T. "Fast Attack Craft." *Navy International* (March 1989): 105–14.

Livezey, William E. *Mahan on Sea Power*. Norman: University of Oklahoma Press, 1947.

Luttwak, Edward N. *The Political Uses of Sea Power*. Baltimore, MD: Johns Hopkins University Press, 1974.

Mabesoone, W. C. "European Cooperation—Naval Lessons from the Gulf War." *NATO's Sixteen Nations* (January 1989). 67–74. "Concerting" the minesweeping effort.

McClintock, Robert. *The Meaning of Limited War*. Boston: Houghton Mifflin, 1967.

Mahan, Alfred Thayer. *The Influence of Seapower Upon History 1660–1783*. American Century Series; New York: Hill and Wang, 1957.

Marder, Arthur J. *From the Dreadnought to Scapa Flow*. 5 vols. London: Oxford University Press, 1965.

Militärgeschichtlichen Forschungsamt. *30 Jahre Bundeswehr 1955–1985*. Mainz: v. Hase & Koehler, 1985.

Milner, Marc. *North Atlantic Run*. Annapolis, MD: Naval Institute Press, 1985. RCN in WWII.

Morison, Samuel Eliot. *The Two-Ocean War*. Boston: Little, Brown, 1963.

Mortimer, John. "Australian Mine Countermeasures Reflect Innovation, Flexibility," *Sea Technology* (November 1989): 18–25.

Naval Review Issue. *U.S. Naval Institute Proceedings* (May 1988). The U.S. Navy in the Persian Gulf.

———. *U.S. Naval Institute Proceedings* (May 1989). The U.S. Navy in the Persian Gulf.

Perry, Hamilton Darby. *The Panay Incident*. New York: Macmillan, 1969. Yangtse, 1937.

Phillips, C. E. Lucas. *Escape of the Amethyst*. New York: Coward-McCann, 1957. Yangtse, 1949.

Porten, Edward P. von der. *The German Navy in World War II*. New York: Thomas Y. Crowell, 1969.

Rabinovich, Abraham. *The Boats of Cherbourg*. Annapolis, MD: Naval Institute Press, 1988. Israeli missile boats of 1973. The birth of EW.

Rogers, Warren, Jr. *The Floating Revolution*. New York: McGraw-Hill, 1962. *Santa Maria*.

Romé (Amiral). *Les Oubliés du Bout du Monde*. Paris: Editions Maritimes & d'Outre-Mer, 1983. Indochina 1939–47.

Rowan, Roy. *The Four Days of Mayaguez*. New York: W. W. Norton, 1975. *Mayaguez*'s seizure and release.

Ruge, Friedrich. *Der Seekrieg*. Annapolis, MD: Naval Institute Press, 1957. Germany's *Kriegsmarine* in WWII.

———. *The Soviets as Naval Opponents 1941–1945*. Annapolis, MD: Naval Institute Press, 1979.

Schull, Joseph. *Far Distant Ships*. Toronto: Stoddard, 1987. RCN in WWII.

Scott, Peter. *The Battle of the Narrow Seas*. New York: Charles Scribner's Sons, 1946. Coastal forces in the English Channel, 1939–45.

Smith, Peter C. *Hold the Narrow Sea*. Annapolis, MD: Naval Institute Press, 1984. Naval warfare in the English Channel, 1939–45.

Sprout, Harold and Margaret. *The Rise of American Naval Power 1776– 1918*. Princeton, NJ: Princeton University Press, 1967.

Steinberg, Jonathan. *Yesterday's Deterrent*. New York: Macmillan, 1965. The Kaiser's navy.

Thomas, Hugh. *The Spanish Civil War*. New York: Harper & Row, 1961.

U.S. Naval Institute Proceedings (October 1989). Special Coast Guard– heavy issue.

Vali, Ferenc A. *The Turkish Straits and NATO*. Stanford, CA: Hoover Institution Press, 1972.

Westcott, Allan. *Mahan on Naval Warfare*. Boston: Little, Brown, 1942.

Young, P. Lewis. "The Sultan of Oman's Navy," *Navy International* (February 1989): 53–58.

Zakheim, Dov S. and Andrew Hamilton. *U.S. Naval Forces: The Peace-time Presence Mission*. Washington: Congressional Budget Office, 1978.

Zumwalt, Elmo R., Jr. *On Watch*. New York: Quadrangle/New York Times Book Co., 1976. High-low mix for the U.S. Navy.

Index

ABOUT THE AUTHOR

CHARLES W. KOBURGER, JR. is a Captain U.S. Coast Guard Reserve, retired in 1978 after twenty years active duty. He is now an independent consultant in the operational aspects of maritime affairs, specializing in navigation systems. Holder of master's degrees in political science and history, he is also a 1965 graduate of the Armed Forces Staff College. In 1983–84, he was the Sir John Cass Fellow at the City of London Polytechnic, working on vessel traffic systems. He has been published many times on both sides of the Atlantic.